BROKEN
BEFORE BATTLE

To James

Live
Life
Full!

Enjoy your
journey!

Thanks for being a fan
+ keep chasing your
dreams!

♡ Aff Howe

To James,

100% is possible,

100% of the time!

D.P.

BROKEN BEFORE BATTLE

CHANGING LIVES
OUTSIDE THE OCTAGON

*James.
Thanks for sharing your
knowledge on life & for taking
care of my family when were in
Vegas. Much love G,
Jeremy Stephen*

SUZETTE HOWE

ShowUhow2MEDIA

Broken Before Battle: Changing Lives Outside the Octagon

Published by ShowUhow2 Media
Tucson, Arizona

ISBN: 978-0-692-12779-7 (paperback)
ISBN: 978-0-692-12897-8 (ebook)
LCCN: 2018906095

Requests for information:
www.SuzetteHowe.com

Cover and Interior Design: Micah Edel
Writing Coach: Adam Colwell
Photography: Courtney Henderson, Jim Burwell

If you're looking to be engaged and inspired, look no further than *Broken Before Battle: Changing Lives Outside the Octagon*. Suzette Howe provides a digestible and valuable look into what it takes for professional athletes to excel at the championship level, even in the face of seemingly insurmountable obstacles. Many of her subjects realize greatness despite conditions that would send most careers sideways and use their circumstances as a source of motivation, and, in the long run, inspiration. Through the eyes of some of the world's best athletes, Howe masterfully chronicles their unique journeys, going right to the source to shine a light on the power of positivity, focus, and self-belief amidst times of chaos, doubt, and uncertainty.

One would be hard-pressed to produce this type of in-depth testimonial without having lived it and seen firsthand what it takes to persevere against the longest of odds. As a parent, there is a lot to be learned from your children. There is no doubt that the triumphs and tribulations of Dominick Cruz have profoundly impacted Howe, his mother, and serve as part of the genesis for this powerful project. There are themes in this book upon which we all can draw in our daily lives and it's not surprising that the woman who produced Dominick would be capable of this important work.

Jon Anik

MMA Commentator

This book is dedicated to everyone wondering if their dream is worth pursing—who desires to be more courageous and disciplined in their goals but are not quite sure how they can achieve their dream because their schedules are full.

To the teachers and coaches who give more of themselves to others through their careers than money will ever return.

To the leaders who are constantly seeking new ways to accomplish teamwork with projects but are questioning how to be refreshed.

To all you "fighters in life" that have triumphed over everyday circumstances and just don't give up. YOU are the difference in your own mind, family, workplace, and neighborhood. Don't ever give up—but *get* up and keep moving forward because you can be victorious and your community needs you!

Foreword

Since I started my professional mixed martial arts career in 2005, I've seen men and women from almost every walk of life strive to make it in this business. Whatever their age, background, or MMA skill set, they all have one thing in common—one truth that resonates in their minds and hearts: Each one is living a double life.

In this book, Suzette Howe takes you behind the bright lights and beyond the hype to share the intimate lives of fighters and coaches—in their words. She helps you see something that I've known for a long time. All of us involved in MMA have a normal life that you're familiar with, filled with everyday stress and responsibilities for home and family. But then we have the fight life—where we add intense training and dieting, six to seven days a week, culminating into a few minutes of defeat or glory in the octagon.

Fighters have two separate lives smashed into one. The hardest part is that everything that happens in the normal life is what makes the fight life more difficult. Being in the gym, dealing with the fight game—that's easy for us. It's in the normal life that we often face our most challenging battles and unexpected triumphs, as you'll learn as you read these in-depth stories.

Broken Before Battle: Changing Lives Outside the Octagon will also show you how each one of us involved in MMA is chasing a dream, a passion, that we're willing to hold on to—no matter what it takes. Yet you may also have a passion you're pursuing, something in this world that's worth fighting for. Just like those of us in the fight game, you might not succeed in achieving that goal and securing the prize, but you're going for it. The testimonies in this book will inspire you to go through the fire to acquire your passion, especially as you meet the fighters and coaches who are willing to live the double life to find and keep their fervor toward their goals.

Finally, this book will introduce you to its author—who also happens to be my Mom. This book is her prize for pursuing her passion and divine calling. She'd never written a book before, but it was something she always wanted to do. She's hitting a new stage in her life, acquiring new goals, and doing things she's always desired to achieve. I want to thank her for continuing to lead the way by example—for never staying stationary but always growing as a human being.

Until I read *Broken Before Battle: Changing Lives Outside the Octagon*, I also had no idea how much I worried her by being a fighter. Yet she never, ever put that on me—and that kept me free to do what I wanted and pursue my dream. I also find it amazing how she took her involvement in my life and career, then created this book from it. Every second she was around me, Mom took in the moment, studied it, and used it to know me and MMA. The book has helped me respect and understand her more than I did before.

I am grateful for her hard work and passion—and I believe you will be, too, as you discover what she reveals about the amazing people featured in this book.

Dominick "The Dominator" Cruz

Two-time UFC Bantamweight Champion
Final WEC Bantamweight Champion

Acknowledgments

I have experienced an amazing journey while getting to know more about mixed martial arts because a longtime dream of mine came true last year: to become an author. I'm grateful to my teachers in elementary and high school who nurtured my drive to write creative stories. Little did I know that I was going to be called to write about some of the bravest warriors on the planet—both inside and outside the octagon!

The testimonies featured in *Broken Before Battle: Changing Lives Outside the Octagon* are told by the fighters and coaches themselves. Because the one-on-one interviews are developed from my personal relationships with them, these novelizations are vulnerable and honest private memories that reveal their dreams, declare their voices, and clarify their hearts to serve others within their community.

A special thanks to each of my friends featured in this book and the truths their stories reveal.

Seth shares how MMA forces him to be a better person and, as a family man, have a positive outlet now when there was nothing positive before in his own upbringing. Phil, meanwhile, explains how an education was difficult, but college prepared him to be an MMA fighter. He had more resources and it prepared him to carefully discern the do's and don'ts in his professional career.

Brendan reveals that what fighters go through to stay ready in training is unachievable by most people. Danny learned how to sacrifice himself as a fighter, but he knew he couldn't leave his family behind just to follow his dream. He had to recognize the need to receive from two different perspectives for his career: family and coaching.

Thom was coaching out of his own experience as an outstanding athlete and wanted to use the same level and model from college sports education to organize MMA competitions in Arizona. Wilson walks us through his childhood eagerness to become a black belt in Brazil and demonstrates consistent drive to be better than ever before.

Jansen explains his amazing development of martial arts training that allows kids who are experiencing extreme difficulty in living situations to trade it out for a healthy mindset in competition with respect, honor, and praise. Roman believes he became a man in high school by literally walking into the gym because it pushed him to limits he didn't know were possible. He knows wrestling workouts develop confidence and pride with toughness to overcome situations in life.

A huge shout out to all the coaches who give countless hours of personal time and energy to their teams and helped my kids and others stay focused on being their best in life. And to my son, Dominick, I am so very blessed because he inspires me as a mother and runs after his dream at all costs. He revealed to me what true endurance and perseverance look like. I tried to encourage my kids by listening between the lines, giving hugs as often as possible when tough times came, and praising them as they pressed through their challenges. All my children are unique in their giftings, and I remind them that being a good leader isn't easy, but it makes others around them better.

My writing coach Adam Colwell has been a godsend in my life as he allowed me to express myself through my words and sometimes challenging thoughts as we wrestled through copy from week to week. Anika, my sweet daughter, has been my confidant and late-night support while Derek, my son and now MMA coach, has added to my martial arts skills by being creative in his teaching and holding me accountable to my goals. My husband Dennis has been gracious, kind, and so supportive through my learning experiences and burning the candle at both ends to accomplish this book while working full time in my own business.

I am blessed beyond measure and can't wait to interview other fighters and their parents and develop the next two books in the series. "Enjoy the journey" is my motto—and indeed I *will!*

Contents

Suzette Howe

PRINCESS WARRIOR WITH A MESSAGE

The excitement of everyone around me is escalating, and I feel my skin tingling as the adrenaline surges through me, spreading warmth all over my body. The faces of those around me are in shadows, illuminated only by the red beacon of exit signs and frequent speckle of cell phones throughout the darkened arena.

I have been here many times before, a place I never imagined I'd be all those years earlier, when I was a single mom working at home and raising my two small boys—one of whom now performs his fierce trade within this very venue and others like it. The pleasant aromas of popcorn and nachos do nothing to offset the excited dread I feel, my appetite dismissed by my mounting nerves as I await the battle. I'm certain the other parents present are just as tense as together we watch for the visually chaotic light fest that seems to be taking forever to begin.

I look at my friend next to me, but she is unaware of my gaze. Her eyes are cast toward the aisle where the next combatant will shortly emerge, cued by loud music and brilliant streams of light from the rooftops, to walk toward the multitude of cameras poised for action. She is just one of over fifteen thousand others anticipating the entrance of the athlete who is about to strut out and command the attention of an entire arena.

Suddenly I am frozen in place as though gripped around the waist by a strongman's grasp—his hold is immovable but kind. My mind's eye is mesmerized as my captor takes me away in a vision to a strange setting, familiar yet unlike anything else I've ever experienced. It, too, is an arena, but it's pitch black, dead silent, and seemingly empty, yet I know thousands of people are present in the vastness of this huge, chilled space. I can't see their faces, but I sense they are all looking forward, their eyes riveted toward the middle of the coliseum. My rapid breathing is all that interrupts this stillness, and my body feels cold and is completely clothed in goosebumps from head to toe.

All at once a piercing flame appears atop one small candlestick. It hovers in the very center of the arena, and the flame leaps joyfully as if trying to break free from the wick.

"What is it?" I whisper, not actually expecting an answer but glad to hear the reassuring sound of my own voice. I peer ahead as the single candlestick mystically moves to light another that appears from nowhere; then the second one is inspired to light a third, and the third inspired to light a fourth, and so on, until a long line of candles stands silently, beaming and floating in the air. The brilliance of the flames causes the darkness to flee, revealing smiles on the faces of all those illuminated by the golden aura that reaches to the rafters.

A deep baritone voice then speaks gently into my ear, and I know with unwavering certainty in my spirit that it belongs to the one who has me in His mighty clench.

"It only takes one light to usher out the darkness and change lives forever. They need to be heard."

Wow! My heart pounds, and I feel the strength of His empowerment flood my soul. Ever since third grade, I've been driven by the dream of living a life of significance through my gifts and talents, yet life has always crowded in with painful trauma and other obstacles thrust upon me to push the dream away and out of reach. But I have continued to overcome and press on because something, or someone, kept drawing me forward with a need to reach out to others and make a difference in their lives.

Now, as I marvel at the flaming candlesticks, and the words of the voice resonate in my mind, I realize that the sport and culture I've been actively involved in for years was going to provide a fulfillment to my dream! As I have been praying earnestly for several of its brave participants, I understand that I am now prepared to use my own life experiences to compassionately listen to those combatants' stories of how they have overcome obstacles great and small and then articulate their personal accounts to bring hope to others. Because of this supernatural experience, I now have a greater purpose for the numerous heartfelt journal entries penned throughout the years and for the countless thoughts and ideas that have been swirling in my mind.

I am going to be the one to share their stories in a way that has never been told before!

And then, just like that, the vision fades away into reality, just in time for me to jump to my feet to the blaring music, with the rowdy crowd cheering and jeering as the next courageous warrior with a story to tell enters the scene from the ground-floor aisle. Walking in stride to his music of choice, the fighter shadowboxes his way through the reaching hands of the audience, being pursued frantically by cameras, to finally arrive to his circle of teammates and cut man waiting to perform their part in this battle preparation.

> *"I am going to be the one to share their stories in a way that has never been told before!"*

This is the way of the octagon—an honorable, valiant, and robust entry into the next fifteen minutes that will foretell this fighting man's future. He is a professional mixed martial arts (MMA) fighter, and through great discipline he has finally arrived at this cage, where real warriors are revealed!

* * *

That vision took place at UFC 178 on September 27, 2014, at the MGM Grand Arena in Las Vegas. It catapulted me deeper into MMA, as I not only watched more fights but increased my own mixed martial arts training to gain a greater understanding of the skill and philosophy each fighter displays in the octagon. I also began to eagerly tap into the fighters, their stories, and the lives they have affected outside the octagon through financial giving and serving in their communities. Finally, as a marketing professional, I was intrigued to learn more about the media's strategy on how and why it covers MMA events.

It's critical that the testimonies featured in *Broken Before Battle: Changing Lives Outside the Octagon* are told by the fighters and coaches themselves. Through my one-on-one interviews with them, forged from personal relationships, their stories will be written as novelizations that declare their voices, reveal their dreams, and disclose their ideas, providing insights that no one else is asking from them.

You'll share their private memories and feel their sincere vulnerability through these honest and personal documentaries. You'll discover the determined mind-set and astonishing benefits that an active discipline in mixed martial arts has given these individuals and others around them. You'll learn that MMA success is not their financial ticket to lifetime security, but that it's their passion to share life-changing concepts through the sport they enjoy that truly motivates them to build a legacy for future generations who are being touched by their influence. In the end, you'll be built up and encouraged to overcome circumstances in your life that may seem beyond your endurance.

I became much more involved than being only a fan of MMA in early 2007, when my son, Dominick Cruz, fought for the first time through World Extreme Cagefighting (WEC), a partner organization of the Ultimate Fighting Championship (UFC). By then he'd been fighting as a mixed martial artist for two years with Total Combat and another organization and compiled a sturdy

9–0 record while earning championship belts in the 145- and 155-pound weight divisions. I attended as many fights as I could at the beginning of his MMA career, yet it wasn't always easy because they took place sporadically and sometimes had last-minute changes regarding when and where the events took place.

My desire to support my son in his endeavors as a young fighter was made more challenging because there were many intricacies I didn't understand about the technique and skill set he needed to participate. Like most kids, Dominick didn't take the time to explain it all to me, but there was no question that I had to find a way to embrace the sport because he became seriously involved right out of high school. While this was a difficult transition as a mom, watching him grind his way through tournaments and matches since he began wrestling in junior high in Tucson, Arizona, made it a little easier.

Dominick became a fighter almost by chance. He was walking around the school campus, out in the hot, dry sun, looking for the soccer coach one afternoon when he saw someone enter a building; he thought they might help him out, so he opened the door and went inside.

"Excuse me, sir," Dominick said, using the manners I'd diligently taught him at home. "Can you tell me where the soccer field is? I want to be on the team."

The man, Coach Edwards, took a long, hard look up and down the skinny, wide-eyed, dark-haired boy in front of him. "Son, you don't look like a soccer player," he said with a knowing smile. "You look like a wrestler to me!"

With that, Dominick was ushered into the sport that was going to change his entire future! At first I thought it was great because he could focus on his education and still participate in a team sport with other kids in his school. He loved the competition and continued to adamantly wrestle his way through opponents and his studies, enabling him to later join one of the top high school squads in the state. I invested countless hours sitting on hard bleachers, watching him compete in sweat-filled gyms and arenas during local meets and tournaments. Tireless road trips to and from events became a way of life for our son and our family. I had just married my second husband, Dennis, when Dominick started wrestling. Jumping into the difficult role of fatherhood for Dominick and his little brother, Derek, Dennis did a terrific job as their stepdad staying involved in their lives. Three years younger than Dominick, Derek was also a student athlete. He played baseball, so we did everything we could to actively participate in each child's sport of choice, even when the schedules conflicted. Our daughter, Anika, a tiny toddler during Dominick's high school years, sweetly melted the hearts of her teenage brothers. She adorably captured the attention of the crowds around us, too, as she learned to climb the bleachers and stadium stairs.

I prioritized meeting with my son's coaches so I could receive vital direction on how to listen to them and not interfere with their instructions for Dominick and Derek. Sadly, these coaches say there are many parents who have never been to a workout, game, or tournament; some haven't even met the coach, even when their child is traveling out of state with the coach. That's a shame. But it's the sacrifices of energy, expense, and time shared by my family and other parents with loved ones who follow their young athletes that creates an amazing bonding time to watch our children's growth and determination.

Some of the lessons I learned early as the mom of a developing fighter were anything but easy. A huge struggle was watching Dominick do whatever it took to maintain his target weight, a requirement before every event to qualify to wrestle with his team. It was a worrisome and grueling process for me, and I had frequent talks with his high school coach, asking about possible nutritional supplements and healthy alternatives because I thought there just had to be a better way—Dominick was always so hungry! It was also tough to see Dominick develop strange, strategic techniques to have the mind-set to cut weight. My heart was torn when he built a shrine constructed with junk food he couldn't eat like cookies, chips, sodas, and sweetened cereals on the desk in his bedroom. Somehow Dominick managed to block out his cravings of these delicacies by insisting that his brother eat them—right there in front of him. Derek hated to do it because it made him feel weird, but he usually obliged his brother out of respect for how hard he was working to keep off the pounds.

Dominick also used "plastics" that are worn beneath clothing to induce severe sweating during his runs in our neighborhood and at school, causing him to be drenched through his clothes. Once I discovered what plastics were and how wearers literally pour sweat out of gathered seams from around their wrists and ankles, I asked Dominick if he was using them. "No, Mom," he lied. "I'm okay. Don't worry about it." He still tells me that same phrase today if he thinks I'm going to stress out. I agonized that his carefree life as a kid seemed compromised by his constant focus on weight, but he loved his sport! The discipline he built as a wrestler made him tough enough to keep moving forward, eager to someday become a champion.

If you're a fan of UFC, then you know Dominick went on to achieve that dream, accruing a combined record of 22-2-0, twice winning the bantamweight title and defending the belt six different times. He was the first ever bantamweight champion when the UFC merged with the WEC in 2010 to grow their divisions and include two more successful lower-weight classes. He continues to further his career as a fighter while advancing as a sports analyst and commentator. He has many stories of trial and triumph, but those will come at a later time in a different book. *Broken Before Battle: Changing Lives Outside the Octagon* is one of three in a forthcoming series devoted to tales of dedication and extreme determination, of people who can be admired and looked upon as mentors to teach the value of long-term sacrifice in order to achieve success.

> *"The discipline he built as a wrestler made*
> *him tough enough to keep moving forward,*
> *eager to someday become a champion."*

*   *   *

As a mother of an MMA fighter, fan of MMA bouts, and an active mixed martial artist, I also desire to reveal the many positive aspects of a sport so often identified with violence and greed. I am astonished by the diversity I see every time I take a seat in an arena, awaiting the next series of fights. People from multiple nations are represented both outside the octagon in the audience and inside the cage with the athletes. Doctors and lawyers, blue- and white-collar workers, plus women and children join the male enthusiasts, who most people assume make up the sport's primary audience. These avid fans are all looking for something to relate to as they watch through the protected lens of distance yet remain engrossed in the captivating exchange of blows before their eyes.

> *"As a mother of an MMA fighter, fan of MMA bouts, and an active mixed martial artist, I also desire to reveal the many positive aspects of a sport so often identified with violence and greed."*

Each person seems to be drawn into viewing and participating by different motivations. Some experience a gratifying release of their everyday anger and aggression as they watch victory and defeat take place on the canvas, almost as if they were the characters themselves in a video game. Others are fighters who engage in the mastery and honor that comes with the sport, evidenced when the combatants offer a hand up at the close of a fight and give their fellow warrior a hug or a pat on the back. As I train in MMA, I experience both sensations while I release aggression on a bag or punch mitts held by an encouraging coach or spar with another willing student of the art. MMA is one sport that demands respect, and most fighters are true gladiators who esteem one another.

Years ago I started training in mixed martial arts through tae kwon do because I wanted to be more prepared and confident in self-defense. I took a class with Anika when she was eleven years old to learn strategic moves to protect myself from an attack, and I quickly discovered I wanted to train more. As a kid, I was active in ballet, tap dancing, and synchronized swimming, so I loved sports and saw MMA as a good way to get back in shape and train my brain to learn new things.

Tae kwon do was difficult because the left and right sides of my body wouldn't coordinate. It was like trying to do a cartwheel leading with the opposite side or striving to write with my left hand when I am right-handed. At times I felt stupid—especially when I watched myself in the mirror during class. But I stayed with it even though I was older and dealt with a variety of nagging, painful injuries. I earned belts as I progressed to the next levels of difficulty in forms, kicks, and sparring, and I grew stronger to excell in high level kicks, eventually earning a brown belt. To this day, I take classes in jiu-jitsu and muay thai kickboxing to round out my skills and thoroughly enjoy mixed martial arts training in addition to work on the treadmill, weight training, and cardio classes.

Tae kwon do jump spinning back kick (left); Jiu-jitsu classic armbar (right)

As a nonprofessional mixed martial artist, I can only imagine how difficult it must be for professional MMA fighters to perform in front of judges and fans. I remember how nervous I was participating in state tae kwon do tournaments in front of a few hundred people; professionals compete in front of thousands, not to mention television audiences that multiply that number. That's fear on steroids! I know what it feels like to have my heart pound rapidly as the adrenaline takes over, potentially leading to serious errors during combat. Sparring against another fighter trying to defeat me requires me to be more agile with my kicks and quicker with my punches to score points and dodge their attack.

Tae kwon do matches are only two three-minute rounds, with thirty seconds of rest in between, and we benefit from the protection of a helmet, chest protector, arm and shin guards, and four-ounce gloves that are far smaller than boxing gloves. Professional MMA fights have three five-minute rounds, with one minute of rest in between, and main event matches are expanded to five five-minute rounds, with nothing for protection other than their gloves. These incredible contrasts enabled me to understand and even feel a small portion of a professional fighter's anxiety, and this insight into their commitment level and discipline has made me an excited admirer of them and the sport we've chosen and love.

Many nonparticipants have told me they can't watch mixed martial arts, because it's too violent, even barbaric. Yet these same people will watch football players slam into each other at full speed or hockey players beat each other up on the ice and deem both to be acceptable entertainment. What they likely don't understand about

MMA is that each fighter is following definite rules that define the sport and are designed to protect them from severe injury. Each combatant is humbly willing and ready to engage in the cage. You'll discover more about the positive aspects of mixed martial arts through the stories of those shared in this book in a way that will revolutionize your view of the sport.

MMA also provides a remarkable opportunity to change the lives of our youth through its skilled athletic training that teaches them a better way to deal with their conflicted emotions. Several of the stories you'll read in *Broken Before Battle: Changing Lives Outside the Octagon* include details about the teaching organizations that fighters actively support in their communities through volunteering or through personal financial gifts and support. Many youths who may become interested in mixed martial arts live in serious situations within their own neighborhoods, where they fight daily to overcome the negative odds of bullying, gang activity, drugs, and violence—all of which are fed by societal pressure to fit in and be part of an accepted group.

Those students are introduced to an entirely new lifestyle when they walk into a gym, studio, or after-school center to learn mixed martial arts. It is a practiced technique that uses combat stances with kicks, elbows, and punches, combined with wrestling and grappling on a mat. By practicing MMA through these intense workouts, these students learn patience, respect, honor, and perseverance, as well as to never fight outside the class unless in self-defense and to never, ever give up. MMA teaches kids to identify with the consequences and realities of lack of confidence, laziness, and inactivity, offsetting them through its physical demands and disciplines of MMA on both the mind and body.

In addition, mixed martial arts are unlike other team sports, where if a player strikes out or misses a tackle, there is a teammate who can make up for the mistake and help the team win. In MMA, if you lose control of your emotions, get mad, or lose your focus, you will lose your match. Combat-type fighting practice brings a team of several people together in a controlled environment where everyone is doing the same training, usually under the direction of one coach. This encourages greater confidence as you train with another teammate, sometimes at your skill level and other times against someone more advanced, and continually improve because of one-on-one interaction. This can be a direct and effective benefit for kids who deal with deeper levels of self-doubt, rejection, or aggression. I have seen numerous youths revolutionized as they experienced greater concentration in their studies, improvements in their behavior, and positive changes in their attitudes.

Commitment to MMA's unique coaching and intense workout routines adds to anyone's character a quality of "sticktuitiveness"— abilities to be on time, to press through, and to strengthen endurance. There seems to be an addiction that comes from participation in mixed martial arts and similar combat sports, such as those previously mentioned and judo, karate, and boxing. It creates positive habits and a desire to better oneself and improve skill levels as you continually compete against your own personal best. Plus, the team atmosphere of all martial arts significantly addresses a young person's inherent need to belong. The stories in *Broken Before Battle: Changing Lives Outside the Octagon* will help you better understand all these realities.

Many of these insights I gained for this book came through being a personal encourager and "second Mom" to some of the professional MMA warriors who train at the Alliance Gym in San Diego, California; All Powers Gym in Stockport, England; and Fight Ready Gym in Scottsdale, Arizona. The sport, its purpose, and its life-changing results captured my heart as I conversed with these athletes and watched some of them practice four hours a day—two hours in the morning and two more at night. I witnessed their radical dedication to a fierce morning regimen of shadowboxing, leg kicks, partner boxing, takedowns, and multiple rounds of sparring. In the evening they followed up with personal strength training through sprints, cycling, weightlifting, and other strategic therapies recommended by their coaches.

Whatever their level of competence or competition, I witnessed both men and women at these gyms experience the camaraderie created through mixed martial arts. Although some members on these teams do not fight professionally, they are experienced sparring partners who attend tournaments or qualify to participate in local fights. Those who are MMA professionals dedicate a greater level of time and body focus to fight within the UFC or other organizations, such as Bellator, Absolute Championship Berkut, World Fighting Federation, and Combate Americas. Their ability to maintain their best strength, mental game, and agility in the center stage of real life while juggling their personal and family responsibilities is truly an expression of determination to be admired—and declared.

> *"Their ability to maintain their best strength, mental game, and agility in the center stage of real life while juggling their personal and family responsibilities is truly an expression of determination to be admired—and declared."*

My mother's heart was filled with compassion, as I was fortunate enough to hear these warriors' stories and discover the legacy each one was yearning to share.

In my vision, they are represented by the individual standing candles, each ignited with a small flame that lit up an entire arena. In real life, they are human beings who willingly fight, sweat, and bleed to overcome mental and physical obstacles to become champions in their own right.

Here are their stories, in their words, and from their hearts.

Seth Baczynski

FAMILY MAN WITH A REAL GRIP ON LIFE

Family is an important part of the life and vitality of MMA welterweight Seth Baczynski, and he carries that big heart for closeness into his everyday relationships with teammates and friends. That's understandable, considering all that he has been through.

Born on the beautiful island of Kauai, Hawaii, Seth remembers running and playing on the beach as a little boy and then hanging out in big luaus with the islanders, who were also all about family—everyone was addressed as aunty or uncle. It was an ideal upbringing, but hardly affluent. Seth was the second youngest of five children, and he and his siblings—Bri, Jeffery, Kaleb, and Isha—all lived together in a blended family. His parents also took care of handicapped children in their home as his father labored in construction. "We could barely feed ourselves," Seth said. "It was a time when people didn't get a lot of money to take care of handicapped kids. My parents did it because they wanted to."

However, the stage was set for tragedy when the national recession of the mid-1980s led to a halt in construction work on Kauai. His father loved Hawaii, but because he was not a native, he wasn't given the same opportunities as the locals when the stock market crashed in 1987. "Things got really tight," Seth said, "so we had to move to Arizona to somehow make a new life."

That's when his parents, overwhelmed by depression resulting from the forced move, became meth users. "My whole family got engulfed in drugs. We moved several times and were the poorest kids in every town we moved to—misfits everywhere we went," said Seth, who was almost six at the time of the move."Plus, our parents fought so loud everyone in the neighborhood could hear them. It was so embarrassing, and all of us kids had a hard time adjusting to our new life in the States."

One positive memory from his tumultuous childhood involved his little sister, Isha. Seth said she had a great sense of humor and was particularly good at mimicking people, especially their father. "Isha would play air guitar the same way Dad did to make fun of him. He always got mad and stomped his feet all the way through our mobile home trailer," Seth said. "We all laughed because she was so funny." Not as positive, though, was Seth's experience with his half-brother, Jeffery, who was five years older and in trouble for as long as Seth can remember. He says Jeffery was respectful of his stepdad and never cussed at their mother even in the most difficult times. "He would look at my brother and me and say, 'Kaleb, go to school and work hard; Seth, go play your sports,' then he'd put us on a bus and go rob a house." Seth shook his head. "He was a good big brother, but sometimes, when my parents were gone, he beat us up. His frustration came from having to act as our parent because they were so messed up. I looked up to him a lot because no matter what, he's my big brother. But he's been incarcerated for life now for more than twenty-six years," Seth said as he stared off in a sad gaze.

"My whole family got engulfed in drugs. We moved several times and were the poorest kids in every town we moved to—misfits everywhere we went."

Not wanting to follow the troubled path of Jeffrey or his parents, Seth used his talent in sports to keep himself out of trouble in elementary and middle school. He was treated well by others because he was a strong athlete. The same, though, was not true in the classroom. "I wasn't good at learning. I never felt stupid, but the hardest thing to understand was why people kept yelling at me because I tried so hard," said Seth. "I was always in trouble, and the teachers couldn't understand why I was so mad. They thought I was just messing around when I got bad grades." In response, Seth was often placed in On Campus Suspension (OCS). "I was inside a white box at a white desk with a chair. The first four or five hours of the day they would bring my work, but they didn't teach me anything. Then they let me out to eat lunch, but that was separate from everyone too. This continued for years. When I got out of the box, I would get wild, and they couldn't understand why I acted like an animal! I did it because I was excited to see people. I remember looking at the teacher and saying, 'I've been in a f***ng box all day,' and then get in trouble for cussing," he said, laughing.

Finally, in his freshman year of high school, a teacher named Kathy Black figured out Seth's problem: he was a narrative dyslexic. "I learn in a story form. If I have to read for myself, I don't understand. But if someone reads a story to me or I watch a movie, I'm good," Seth said. "All the teachers throughout my education talked down about me, but I made it through because I was a great athlete. I think I could have done better in school, but to the credit of a few teachers and coaches who took time to work with me and saw something in me, I graduated."

In 2001, Seth graduated from Apache Junction High School east of Phoenix where he competed in basketball, football, and track. "I 'street fought' a lot, too, growing up. You have to have a good sense of humor when you're that poor, and you gotta know how to fight," said Seth. It was a few years after graduation when a buddy who was an MMA fighter, Brandon Oliver, or "Little B," invited Seth to coach him in his corner during a small-town fight. "Little B was a terrible fighter, but he had fun and liked to scrap, so he told me, 'Come in here, and we'll whoop all these guys your size!' I loved competing, and even though I had confidence because I had gained some weight and was bigger from working out, I didn't put much into the idea of being a fighter," said Seth. "Yet it did inspire me to go take one jiu-jitsu class, and four days later I fought. I fell in love with it and have been doing it ever since."

Martial arts inspired Seth so much as a young man that he tells moms who ask about bullying or self-defense to put their kids in wrestling while they are young in school. "They can take down good strikers; then you don't have to watch them get punched and kicked in the face! It's scary out there, so if they take wrestling, no matter who they have coming at them, they can take them down," Seth said, hitting his fist on the table. "Kids get their butts beat, and it takes years off their life if they don't learn this stuff." He told his eleven-year-old son, Skyler, the same thing, and he's taking an interest in wrestling. "But I'm gonna do him 'one-up' because my coach was once Pac-Ten coach of the year, and I used to train with him at a gym where there was a judo gold medalist too. So I'm taking my son three days a week to wrestling and two days a week to judo classes that will give him a different attack in takedowns," he said. "When I told my son, 'Take judo,' and he asked me why, I said, 'You can be losing a wrestling match with two points and then throw someone and get five points to win.' My son said, 'I want to go tomorrow!'"

Seth believes that any kid can gain confidence by getting involved in sports. "Winning was great and losing sucked, but the friendships, coaches, and people taking an interest in me encouraged me to live differently," he said. "But there's no glory in wrestling; it's a difficult, grinding workout with sweaty mats and teammates. You have to watch how you eat, stay disciplined, continue to get good grades, and make weight in order to fight." He added there was also no popularity in wrestling, either, when he was younger, because girls didn't want to talk to him. "Now that I'm fighting professionally, girls actually want to talk to me. But I'm good," he said with a big grin.

*   *   *

Near the beginning of his career, Seth worked with Arlene Sanchez-Vaughn, a professional fighter since 1984 and current striking coach for all competitors for FIT NHB mixed martial arts in Albuquerque, New Mexico. Back then, most fighters didn't have female coaches, but Seth heard from well-known cut man Rob Monroe that she was working with longtime MMA fighter and former WEC welterweight champion Carlos Condit. "She was straightforward and abrupt, so her nickname was 'Knarly'—we got along that way," Seth said. "Coach Arlene would say, 'One, two, and stomp with your leg! Jose Aldo does it right.' She made me kick a bag for three hours, but she was excellent. I enjoyed training with her and respect her as a coach."

Knarly's training prepared Seth well. After more than ten years as a professional fighter in two different weight divisions, Seth has his battle scars among them—a broken arm from an armbar, a broken nose, and surgery on his ACL. He's proven himself a diligent competitor, with a record of 20–14 in a variety of organizations worldwide, including two stints in UFC, where he earned a pair of Fight of the Night honors and was included in two different seasons of *Ultimate Fighter*. His great-grandfather was Polish and the inspiration for Seth's nickname, the Polish Pistola. It fits him well, as he keeps pointing forward, aiming to always be a finisher in the sport; he definitely possesses a warrior's heart.

Of course, Seth's heart for family often extends to his teammates inside the octagon as well. "When my friends fight in the arena, I want to cry sometimes because I'm so scared for them. When I'm cornering for them and walk out with them to their music, I think, 'Oh man, I can't believe I'm doing this!' But when I fight, I don't think about it—I love competing and everything about MMA," said Seth. "But the hardest thing about being a pro athlete is dealing with life. As crazy as that sounds, there's never been anything in the cage that frightened me. But having five kids and knowing the kind of life I grew up in—that responsibility still scares me."

Seth worked hard for many years to change the type of person he was after he met his fiancée, Taylor, and then started his own family. "Instead of being comfortable with myself, I remember running away from everything. People made fun of my family, and they looked down on us at the grocery store. I hated that look of pity and sorrow," he said, grimacing in disgust. "I tried to alter who I was through the process of growing up, but I learned later that the hardest thing I had to overcome was me and my thoughts. Without a doubt, I can be my best asset but also my worst enemy. I had to concentrate on not self-destructing and letting go of things I couldn't control. Even though I am strong-willed, sometimes I can be incredibly weak."

Yet Seth also knows the two or three hours a day he spends in training—hitting mitts and learning his sport—means he is building relationships he will have for the rest of his life. "The people I've met, like Dominick Cruz, seeing so many places I would never have gone, and doing so many cool things—that's what drives me," he said. "It forces me to be a better person and gives me a positive outlet with my family now where there was never anything positive before. It was turmoil for so long, not knowing why my family was the way they were or what was wrong and having that uncertainty. But in MMA and training, I have certainty. It gives me something to put my energy toward instead of drinking, womanizing, or being a jerk. There were so many things I did out of spite as a very unhappy person, but now I have something that allows me to sleep at night."

"It forces me to be a better person and gives me a positive outlet with my family now where there was never anything positive before."

That sense of certainty has allowed Seth to focus on ways he can give back. For example, he and a couple of friends volunteered to offer student-athlete seminars on diet and improving overall health at Seth's old high school in Apache Junction. "Sustainable nutrition can help kids achieve their goals, from passing pre-college tests and earning scholarships to making weight for that state championship they want. They can be healthy for the whole season so they don't burn out and lose their 'win' about maintaining their body," Seth said. "I tell them, 'Nutrition is like gasoline in a vehicle. If you were a truck going up a hill and you have no gas, you won't make it up the hill. You have to put the right fuel into your body and be like high octane—the best you can be. Being a high-profile athlete is one big sacrifice after another.'"

In 2014 Seth was also selected to participate in a fighter Tour for the Troops sponsored by the United Service Organization. He enjoyed providing MMA training at the army and air force bases they visited on the Azores, a group of islands over 900 miles from Lisbon, Portugal. He and the other fighters taught moves such as a double-leg takedown, how to get past an opponent's guard, and various head and arm chokes. Seth and a fellow fighter taught one such technique called the "rear naked choke" to a few of the airmen. "One of the guys had jiu-jitsu training and was doing the move with the hand on top of the head, pressing down. He was a big guy, so I showed him how to turn up its effectiveness by placing the back of his hand to press against the back of his opponent's head near his ear, leaning back and squeezing at the same time. 'You'll put him out,' I told them."

It turned out that the airman, Spencer Stone, likely used that very technique to subdue a terrorist on a train in France in 2015, saving many lives. "I tell people all the time, 'You can train in boxing or other fighting that's not MMA, but if a guy has a gun, he can kill you. You may have only one chance to save your life and someone else's,'" Seth said. "Learning how to apply the actual skills that you might need someday—it's what mixed martial arts can do. Spencer is a great example of this because everyone was going to die on that train. People say this sport is barbaric, but it's more ignorant to think you're untouchable or that you will never be a victim. Spencer was prepared. I've told my son, 'It's going to be your job as a young man to learn how to protect your family as an adult.'"

> *"I tell people all the time, 'You can train in boxing or other fighting that's not MMA, but if a guy has a gun, he can kill you. You may have only one chance to save your life and someone else's."*

*　　　*　　　*

Seth believes it's important to shed light on a couple of prevalent issues in MMA. "I think some situations about domestic abuse involving mixed martial arts fighters are not covered correctly in the media because it's just as bad in other competitive sports," he said. "Those who are guilty of abuse have to do a better job at not putting themselves in that position because one bad scene ruins it for the whole bunch. Truth is, some women prey on professional athletes, especially men who are already angry because they have been washed out of this sport. That's never an excuse to abuse someone, but that is a reality."

Another frustration for MMA fighters, Seth said, is that they are grossly underpaid. "We should be compensated similar to other athletes in major sports because we have much of the same full-time training obligations," he said. "Some fighters put their bodies through five-round fights with full camps and only get the purse of a three-round fight. We don't make enough money to take care of our bodies the way we need to perform at the level we're demanded. We don't have the facilities and benefits like they do in the NBA and NFL, with trainers, dieticians, or bonus money. We have nothing like that supplied and must invest in that care for ourselves, so we often take whatever options we are given to earn income through a fight."

The opportunity came up for Seth to be featured again in the UFC's *The Ultimate Fighter: Redemption series*, and although it was low pay for the fight, and he didn't get the win, Seth is still happy with the results. He finished his medical respite mid-2017 after an ACL surgery and said, "I want to put every piece of me into this. Bellator is better for pay, but still, what you think you're worth is not gonna happen. Natural-born will is stubbornness that doesn't give up—sometimes to a fault. Very few people understand the trauma our brains and body go through and what it costs for being the best. I know how much Dominick has been through; he's awesome and helped me big time during my ACL recovery. I would complain about my pain or situation and remember, 'Oh yeah, Dominick has been through this three times. What am I crying about!' He's one of the biggest reasons I can't let my last two professional fights stay where they are."

All that said, Seth tries to keep things in perspective. "Life's a process. You can never go back in time, and you can't get any restarts," he said. "There have been times when I've made dumb decisions, but I don't let money issues control my life because money is not what I'm going to think of when I finally close my eyes. I'm going to see my kids, friends, and family. Those are going to be the faces that flash before me. It's not going to be my bank account number."

> *"We don't make enough money to take care of our bodies the way we need to perform at the level we're demanded. "*

*   *   *

Determined to keep family a priority, Seth kept his heart open to sister Isha as she struggled with alcohol and drug abuse. He did the best he could to help her children, Rylee and Jordan, as they grew up with drama and turmoil in their home. Seth once told himself that if he was ever in a position to help any kid or family member to grow up in a better situation, he would do it. "Isha was a loving person when we were kids, and I was always the one in trouble," Seth said. "Whenever I ran away, she brought me clothes and was sincerely concerned. She really cared about me."

But Isha continued with her addictions. One day the police were taking her into custody. Though Rylee was with her stepfather, Kevin, she asked the police to call Seth. "Can you pick Rylee up from Kevin today by six?" the officer asked. "Otherwise, we're taking her into custody with Child Protective Services." Seth didn't hesitate and agreed to meet with Kevin. "Later, when he arrived, Rylee got into my car, but Kevin took her sister, Jordan, with him," Seth said. "When I asked Rylee if she was okay and what had happened, she told me, 'My parents kept on fighting, so the cops came and took Mom to jail. Then Kevin told me, 'You have to go with Uncle Seth because we're going to a family reunion—and you're not family.' When Rylee told me that, I remembered as a kid how everyone treated us. It really made me mad. But I was glad to help Rylee during that time when everyone else went to the reunion."

It wasn't too long afterward that Seth was indeed placed in the position to do much more for his niece. "Isha was still struggling with addiction," he said, "wolves or demons inside her, and she was so lost." She was at a bar buying drugs when there was an altercation. She was fatally shot by the police, who, Seth said, reported that she didn't cooperate with them. "The way they represented her when she died was really not her. I knew who she was before all this," he said. "Nobody wants to die from a drug overdose, or the way my sister did. The hardest part is that the person who dies isn't really the one you knew; there's no way to change it or go back in time. No one—parent, brother, or friend—wants that as the last memory of that special someone. It's a terrible thing to go through."

The police then called to ask Seth if he wanted to take Rylee again—for good. He didn't give it a second thought, but he was nervous to ask Taylor if it was okay with her. "I called my wife. Taylor responded, 'So I'm making her a plate for dinner?' She didn't say 'this isn't our problem' or anything like that. We just brought her home to be with us, and we've had her as part of our family ever since." My brother Kaleb adopted Jordan, and the sisters still keep in touch and go camping together." Seth added, "Every now and then I see Isha in Rylee through a certain look she gives or the way she moves, and I think, 'There's my sister, even though she's gone.' Rylee was the best thing that could happen out of a superbad situation."

Another best thing to happen in Seth's life was when he met Taylor thirteen years earlier. "She's so loving and smart, tough but stubborn—plus beautiful inside, too, not just on the outside," he said. "My family didn't show love to each other, so expressing love was hard to get used to. I didn't even know how to act with her family at first. It took a lot of time to forget what *I thought* family was like and see what family really is. They have such a way as a family—singing 'Johnny Appleseed' and celebrating Christmas. It's a wonderful time." Seth thought her parents would hate him because they worked at the same middle school he attended. "I was such a bad student, but they put up with me now," he said, grinning.

"And remember the principal who put me in OCS? We're friends now, and I see him every Thanksgiving and Christmas! And the teacher I hated all my life now sticks up for me and says, 'Seth never lied to me.' I dress just like that teacher for those family events—in khakis and a polo. I think it's fun."

> *"Nobody wants to die from a drug overdose, or the way my sister did. The hardest part is that the person who dies isn't really the one you knew; there's no way to change it or go back in time."*

Seth, Taylor, and their children—Skyler, Rylee, Alex, Degan, and Sunshine—live in a beautiful ranch home in the Phoenix area that they affectionately call the Funny Farm. They have two dogs, several cows and bulls, turkeys, roosters, pigs, goats, and lots of chickens. They make for an active and playful home setting. "To see my kids as close as they are and to watch how much they love each other and spend time together is amazing. The sweet things they do for each other that me and my brothers and sisters never did as kids have affected me a great deal," Seth said. "When I'm done fighting, I will continue to go to my kids' games, go on camping trips, and have a little extra income to enjoy with the people I love in my life. It's so good to know as a dad that if I died tomorrow, there are still five good human beings on this earth."

Phil Davis

*STRONG AND DETERMINED,
YET FULL OF COMPASSION*

For Phil Davis, who became Bellator light heavyweight champion in November 2016 after a successful five-plus-year stint in UFC, one of his greatest battles did not come in the octagon but before he even decided to become a professional mixed martial arts fighter.

The Harrisburg, Pennsylvania, native was attending college on a wrestling scholarship at home-state powerhouse Penn State University when that battle was fought in his mind. And considering that he was a four-time NCAA all-American who finished with an individual title and an overall wrestling record of 116–15, it's a battle you'd never expect him to encounter.

"The first three-and-a-half, four years in college I had that question mark in my head. People said, 'You just don't know if you have a chin. You have to wait till you get hit to know if you have a chin.'" The question continued for Phil as he graduated and began training with the Lion Heart MMA team in State College, Pennsylvania, and even persisted after he took his first blow. "It's one of those weird things that holds you back," Phil said. "But for me, the 'What if I don't fight?' question outweighed the danger of regard for my personal safety. I thought it was the right move, and I prayed about it for a long time."

Phil's determined faith developed from his parents and upbringing in an active church community, where he attended services every Sunday and found friends to hang out with him and his brothers, Geoffery and John. Even though his parents divorced when Phil was five years old, they still acted lovingly toward each other and fostered a great relationship with him. When he eventually moved out of his mother's home as a young adult, he looked for the same type of loving church community where he could continue his new life on his own.

When Phil and his brothers were young, they fought a lot, but in a good way. They spent all their time together after school and during the summer months, so it was only a matter of time before two of them got into a fight while the other played referee. "It didn't matter what we were fighting about—a Mario card or something like that—but we only wrestled. We didn't start using weapons until later on. My brothers and I are still fairly close as adults, and it's funny, but Geoffery always calls to give me a new take on things before a fight. I listen even though he's not a fighter. He's my big brother and feels that he can lead me on the path to victory," Phil said, smiling.

Phil began wrestling when he was in the eighth grade, and by the time he was a team captain at Harrisburg High School, he was also competing in tennis and cross-country running. Phil's parents worked together to facilitate transportation and support so he could excel at sports as a young athlete. They drove him from one place to another and sat in gymnasiums to support their son. "One time my dad drove from Pennsylvania to North Dakota to see my big wrestling tournament for high school. He likes to be a big fan and didn't want to miss a minute of it," Phil said. "It was a crazy thing to do, driving his car there in the dead of winter, but when our coach bus from Pennsylvania to Iowa broke down, he asked if I wanted to drive back home with him. It was a long trip, but definitely quality time spent."

Phil's parents also encouraged him when learning seemed far more difficult for him than for most of his fellow student athletes. "I don't talk about it much, but I am dyslexic," Phil said. "They discovered this while I was in the fourth grade, when everything I did just needed more time to accomplish, and I was a very slow reader." Dyslexia is a learning disorder characterized by difficulty reading because the letters and words become mixed up or transposed. It took intentional work from his parents to help Phil read more often, and he said there isn't a Goosebumps book that he hasn't read. "They were the coolest thing, and scary too! Children need to find that the idea of school is not boring; it's just they need to discover a way to connect with learning," Phil said. "After the Goosebumps series of books, I read everything nature and science related. Looking back, my learning challenges were good for my family."

Entering college, Phil knew it was going to take far more effort to read, study, and remain focused to accomplish his degree in five years compared to other students. "I remember thinking how tough it was trying my best to get good grades, and all the while I have a full-time job of being on the wrestling team. I had to compete in school against students that didn't have a learning disability, and whose only area of profession was in the classroom," Phil said. "Even though it doesn't ruin my life or stop me from reading books or educating myself, it slowed the process down—and it definitely put a chip on my shoulder."

> *"Children need to find that the idea of school is not boring; it's just they need to discover a way to connect with learning."*

It frustrated Phil that he couldn't read all his course materials in one sitting or focus for a long period of time to get his academic work done. A competitive person, he wanted to be as good as any of his classmates or wrestling teammates. Phil imagined taking the average student and putting them through two wrestling workouts—one in the morning before school, and another team training session with grappling in the afternoon—while attending classes all day in between, five days a week. He believes they wouldn't have the energy to take care of everyday tasks very well, much less meet their classroom responsibilities. "In addition to practice, all the extra requirements of cutting pounds through strict diet to stay in your weight classification, having intense pressure on your body during workouts, and lifting weights, while concentrating on your studies, are required daily in this sport."

Phil kept the same never-give-up mentality he had for sports and brought it into the classroom when he needed extra help but wasn't always able to admit it. "Sometimes I studied to the point of calling out, 'Forget it! God, please do something here! I would rather just take a bad grade than deal with the fact that it's taking me much longer to read this book!'" But a few teachers gave him direction academically by helping him create goals that peaked his interest in things that fascinated him. While he had several great teachers in college, Phil identified his ethics of sports teacher, Dr. Lally, as being significant. "He's a triathlon runner, and together, with his wife, really understood me because he was an intense athlete. They acknowledged my mentality toward athletics and knew that every level of motivation is different for people who are active or involved in sports. He was able to help direct me professionally and career wise as well," he said.

Phil, however, knows that he may not have successfully tested into Penn State, so he's grateful he earned a scholarship to open the doors to college. "I don't want to put it out there that I was a dummy, but I believe it took far more effort compared to anybody else," he said. "But if you have a learning disability, it's not the end of the world." He continues to apply that overcoming attitude in MMA. "I don't like weakness and don't like excuses, so I've trained myself in sports to never have an excuse for failure and to never have an excuse for losing or giving up points in a match or positions to my aggressor."

Working through those difficulties with dyslexia taught him the advantage of an education. "If a kid were to come ask me about becoming a fighter, I'd say the best thing is to try to get some education out of the way, go to college, and if they still want to be a professional fighter, then do it," he said. "In a lot of ways, college prepared me to be an MMA fighter; it gave me more resources and prepared me to sift through the dos and don'ts of the professional arena. There's so much value in learning, and if you can go to school and wrestle or just go to school and study, I feel an education gives you more options both as a fighter and as a professional."

Phil says he remains a goal-oriented person and focuses on his profession with the same intensity as he did on education, which gives him the personal discipline that pushes him in his career. As part of that focus, Phil's had the privilege of being called upon by other fighters to help them train in preparation for big fights. He was asked by former opponent Alex Gustafsson to travel to Sweden to work with him in advance of Alex's bout against Glover Teixeira, a fighter Phil had previously defeated. "It's a humbling feeling knowing in terms of this world that you're valuable to others who want to be good fighters," Phil said. "Bringing in a former opponent to train with you in camp is unique from any other sport. It's as if you're an engineer and specialist in your field; making someone else better through your particular skill set is a wonderful experience," said Phil.

Phil also uses self-accountability that he learned as a student to drive his growth as an athlete and has frequent introspective talks with himself. "I find out what I want to fix to get myself moving forward. Then I say, 'Hey, can I do something different about this next time? Maybe I just need to have some encouragement to do it better.'" Phil will then ask his coach for input and apply this principle in training. He feels like if he's not prepared, it's almost compulsive; he has to go and train. "I have to get better. I just don't like standing still—and I definitely don't like losing," Phil said. "It's the same thing outside the octagon, but the stakes are higher. I'm married and have children now; there's not really an option to lose at life, so that's what motivates me."

"Bringing in a former opponent to train with you in camp is unique from any other sport. It's as if you're an engineer and specialist in your field; making someone else better through your particular skill set is a wonderful experience."

*   *   *

Phil said it's hard for him to have quality relationships because so much of his time as a professional athlete is not his own. When he's at the gym, there are a lot of missed calls and unanswered text messages and voice mails, but his friends know the value of his friendship. "It's hard; you gotta know you're my buddy. I may not talk to you for a week, but after that we're talking all the time. My closest friends get it," he said, "but I've lost some really good friends because I'm not mindful of birthdays and holidays." Sometimes others have called Phil at unknowingly inconvenient times, like the day of a fight when he won't take any calls unless they're important. "I'm my own boss, and I have to run a tight ship. Near fight time, my friends and family will say, 'Hey, good luck, buddy,' and I appreciate it, but it doesn't always get answered."

> *"It's the same thing outside the octagon, but the stakes are higher. I'm married and have children now; there's not really an option to lose at life, so that's what motivates me."*

Another challenge Phil faces as a professional fighter is money management, but he's developed an interesting perspective on money that he applies to discipline himself when spending it. He used to buy all kinds of shoes simply because he wanted them and could afford as many as he desired. But he became concerned that money might become a vice, so he always asks himself if or why he needs something before buying it.

"I hear silly adages like 'money changed you' or 'you're different now because you have money,' but I believe real change should be happening in life regardless of money. Some people expect you will have the same relationship with them or the same interests throughout your life, but that's unreasonable," Phil said. "As you grow older, you change along with your life vision. That can draw you away from an old crowd. Money *should* change you, and I'm careful choosing friends because it can be costly."

Quality friendships are important to Phil, as are spiritually minded people who move toward kindness and sharing their faith by serving the less fortunate. "I frequent a Panera Bread restaurant, and one of the managers there asked me if I'd be interested in putting together a Thanksgiving dinner event to serve the homeless and needy in our community. I said, 'Absolutely!' And the weird thing was my family and friends all had something planned for that day, but I did it anyway," Phil said.

The following year he brought in additional friends to help, and after two years the event grew to benefit more than nine hundred people, with everything being donated. He says it's been a blessing to be part of an influential team of people who can "… create something from nothing. It's a special gift from God to make this happen. We're going to be busy serving every Thanksgiving Day because it just feels right to give back," Phil said. "I didn't do mission stuff as a kid, but I have learned to use my gifts as a tool for God's Kingdom."

Phil also participates in a special mission trip each year to the Dominican Republic. "It's awkward to explain because I have a lot of friends who go there for vacation, and when people hear me say I'm going to the Dominican Republic, they say, 'Wow, that's gonna be awesome!' I come back with, 'Oh no, I'm not going to *that* part of the island. I'm going to the *other* side.'" Smiling, Phil admitted that he's a skeptic and didn't want to be part of a scam, but nevertheless trusted the special program through his church to give thirty dollars per month to send a kid to a Christian school in the Dominican Republic. Each sponsored child also received meals and multivitamins. "Many kids are so poor that's the only meal they get," Phil said, "and I liked the idea of them receiving faith through education."

When given the opportunity to go with the man who organized the charity to the Dominican Republic and meet the children he was financially supporting, Phil couldn't pass it up.

"He emailed me a scribbled drawing from a child and mailed me a picture of him, and at first I wondered how many other people got the same thing," Phil said. "But because I want to be involved physically and not just financially, I went down to meet the two little boys with their family. They were so thankful, and I could see—and was one hundred percent sure—this was not a scam. The whole thing was touching."

Phil was a single dad at the time. "The boys' father asked me, 'Where is your wife? Is it just you?' I responded, 'Yes, it's just me.' He said, 'You sponsored us by yourself and you took the time to come here? Thank God for you!' He was practically crying. You just can't fake that level of gratitude; it's so real in my heart, and it was something I had to do," Phil said. "Many things were difficult to express in communication, and they speak only Spanish, but the message was crystal clear. You don't need a translator to convey those emotions. As a parent, I can only imagine what it would feel like to be on the other side of the table and have a stranger do something for my child that I couldn't provide."

Because he met the family at a special ice cream social event put on by the ministry, Phil didn't get to see the family's actual home or neighborhood, but the father detailed how hard he worked and how expensive school was. He then said of one of his sons, "I think my kid's going to be an engineer." Phil added about the child and family, "He's super ultrabright, and his parents have education at the forefront of their values. They also went to a church locally, so they're believers in the Lord. I believe the school thing is really secondary to everything else we were experiencing together as brothers and sisters in Christ."

The missions outreach, called Go Sports Ministry, now receives the support of Phil's family. "Our little ones don't go yet, but it will be a wonderful experience in the future," he said, adding one of the things that makes marriage so special to him is what his wife and children do together as a family. "I sacrifice myself for her, and she sacrifices for me, but we both do it jointly for other people and the common cause," Phil shared. "I'm also excited, too, because Go Sports Ministry was on my shorts and banner for my big fight at Madison Square Garden. I felt like it was one of the biggest fight stages yet; how perfect it was to have this ministry team represented there."

*　　　*　　　*

In September 2015, Phil left UFC to join Bellator because he could pursue sponsorships and increase the likelihood to win a title in Bellator's tournament format. In Bellator fighters are given title shots based solely on their performances, versus UFC's divisional structure, where fighters face each other based on how many fights they've won or the perceived quality of the other opponent. There is also more rest time between bouts, he says, because Bellator has half the competitors UFC does.

Now considered a fight game veteran, Phil has often been asked if he wants his sons involved in fighting. "That's a weird thing to want for someone else. I wouldn't want to wish the stress of being the president of the United States on my child, but I'd say, 'You can do whatever you want to do. If you want to be the president, I'll help you.' Yet I wouldn't begin that process *for* him; you don't know fully who your child's going to be, and you want kids to make a decision on their own," Phil said. "There's a lot that goes into fighting professionally, including personality type, time dedication, and it's best to have the physicality for it. If you force fighting on the wrong person—maybe God made them to be a bookworm, but you see them as Muhammad Ali—he's going to get beat up! I couldn't live with thrusting that on anybody's child. So I don't want my son to be a fighter, but if that's what he chooses to do," he said, his face beaming with a determined smile, "I'll make sure he's *really* good at it."

Phil believes parents have a definite role in their children's future no matter what sport or activity their child pursues, adding that he can sympathize with what it would feel like as an MMA mom to see his son competing in mixed martial arts. "There's obviously some danger to this sport, but most parents don't worry about cuts, scratches, and black eyes as much as they worry about the big injuries," Phil said. "I'm not saying that big injuries cannot happen, but what you *see* when you're watching MMA seems a little bit more dangerous than what I *feel* and is actually happening inside the cage as a fighter. People are conditioned to see blood as proof of imminent death. They'll say, 'Oh, he's bleeding. He's cut from his eyes. He's gonna die soon,'" he said, laughing. "But in our sport, it's usually a superficial injury that causes a lot of blood but not serious trauma. It is dangerous as a professional in this sport, don't get me wrong. But it's not quite as bad as it looks."

Phil remembers what his father first said to him when he revealed he wanted to be an MMA fighter. "'You're crazy!' he told me. 'You're gonna end up a vegetable, son. Someone's gonna break your neck; then who's gonna take care of you?' That was his knee-jerk reaction, but he showed a real concern. I'm not saying that I'm not crazy; you have to be a little crazy to do what I do," Phil explained while raising an eyebrow. "But we had to go over what happens in the sport, and I explained safety to him regarding referees and the rules inside the octagon. Now he's totally cool with it, but I don't fault him for trying to talk me out of it."

Phil's mother also follows his career and attends most of his fights. "She's a trooper. I'm glad that I came from wrestling first before entering MMA because the idea of just straight-up brutality was a little bit too much for her, but she understands it a little better and doesn't get too squeamish about watching me fight," Phil said.

Parents whose sons or daughters are involved in martial arts should try training in the sport, Phil believes, to gain a greater knowledge of and appreciation for the physical competition. "They don't have to spar or actually fight with another student of the art," he said, "but they can participate in a class and learn what happens in training so they have a better understanding of the sport while watching the bouts or matches."

A huge benefit of that understanding, Phil says, is the recognition of what is real and what isn't. "When watching movies containing fight scenes, there are guys on TV like Liam Neeson who come into a room and beat up four guys all at once. He's my father's age and beating up four guys; it's not real life," Phil said, adding that others watch pro wrestling on TV with the same misconception. "Wrestlers do take a beating, but they are far to the south on the fake side. There's a stunt coordinator orchestrating the action. It's comedy, not real competition," Phil said.

> *"Everybody thinks you have to have violent feelings, but I believe the exact opposite. What people see in the streets is violent, but this is an athletic competition."*

Mixed martial arts combat is 100 percent real, Phil said, but he's careful to point out that when fighters portray a bad guy with a violent persona to try to sell their fight, that doesn't mean that's who they really are or that they intend serious harm or permanent damage to their opponent. "Would Conor McGregor really try to paralyze my son or daughter if they were professional fighters inside the cage? I doubt it—but he is a *real* fighter," Phil said. "I don't think boxing professional Floyd Mayweather is a bad guy, either, and I bet those who know him like him. But he sells this image of a bad guy, even when he's not competing. Not everything you see on TV is real; as fighters, we are not always free to be ourselves. Fans shouldn't assume they know who someone is by public performance alone."

When Phil is interviewed or appears in prefight events, he is respectful, presents a huge smile, and is positive. However, he says he's actually shy. "But God hasn't given me a shy position in the

MMA world, so I have to be a little more outgoing than I want to be," Phil said. "I'm an introvert, but I do enjoy being around people." Phil also struggles to understand the value of the insincere hype and drama of combatants talking back and forth in the days building up to an event. "It's unnecessary," he said. "Once I sign the contract and we've agreed to participate in a professional fight, it seems completely pointless to me to go through all those dramatic emotions, but that's how fights are sold through the media entertainment industry." While he can see how the theatrics help some viewers fulfill their desire to live vicariously through the sport and its personalities, when he watches MMA or any other sport, it's all about the competition. "I tune in just to watch who will win," he said. "I can turn on a football game halfway through because I'll get to see what I want to know: who will win. It's the same thing with tennis. I don't need a story line or back and forth drama," Phil said.

That mind-set was challenged in Phil's MMA battles with Ryan Bader. In college Phil wrestled against Ryan and defeated him, denying him a national title. In MMA, however, Ryan beat Phil in a closely contested UFC fight two-and-a-half years later. Then Phil became Bellator's light heavyweight champion. He put his title on the line against Ryan, who had also become part of Bellator, and Phil lost the rematch and his title. "If I were to harbor feelings that are not good, I have to let it go outside of the ring," Phil said. "Everybody thinks you have to have violent feelings, but I believe the exact opposite. What people see in the streets is violent, but this is an athletic competition. I pray for me and pray for the other guy because I want it to be good, fun competition and don't want anyone to get hurt."

In late 2017, Phil pounded his way through to an impressive win over Leo Leite, taking his record to 18–4–1. Whether it's his ability to take a punch, capability to overcome a learning disorder, or capacity to give back to others less fortunate than him, Phil Davis never shies away from a challenge. He seeks to live with tenacious authenticity driven by genuine faith. It's a story line that Phil knows is still being written. "As much as I would love to script this journey and know where it will go, leave it up to God—He does a better job planning my life than I do. I enjoy fighting, I love competing, and I would love for part of my skills as a fighter to translate into a number of things. But we shall see what happens."

Brendan Loughnane

*ON A TENACIOUS JOURNEY,
ALWAYS BATTLE READY*

Some fighters are well known for their big fights in the big lights. Others show themselves victorious through great wins in the octagon because they are consistently battle ready.

Brendan Loughnane is *that* kind of fighter. A featherweight champion in Tanko Fighting Championship, with a record of 15–3–0, Brendan is Irish; hails from Manchester, England; and is notorious for the wild, persistent passion he brings to every match. He's always ready to fight on a moment's notice while awaiting his opportunity to surpass his popularity in the United Kingdom and to achieve international recognition as a top fighter.

Brendan brawled through the amateur ranks with five wins in two years—each one was characterized by him coming right out and rushing his opponents, fiercely punching from varied stances, and dealing out unforgiving kicks with power that entertained crowds across the United Kingdom. Just after taking the win in his professional debut with X-treme Kombat in June 2010, he went to Malia, Greece, with his friends for three weeks to celebrate. "We're all partying, drinking, and relaxing, and one of my friends said, 'Hey, guys, you want to go watch an MMA show?' We went to this outdoor venue at a beautiful beach setting, where we were all having a good time," Brendan said. "Then we heard an announcement: 'Sorry, everyone, the main event is off tonight. One of the fighters has pulled out.' I said to my buddies, 'Oh *really*,' with a big smile on my face. 'I'll take that fight.'"

His friends tried to talk Brendan out of it; the opponent was thirty-five pounds heavier and a defending champion. But Brendan was determined. "The promoter looked me up and down and thought I was insane. I had pink beach shorts on and that was it," he said with a smirk. Brendan went into the dressing room, and his friend, who didn't know much about MMA, stood in front of Brendan, holding the striking pads so he could practice sparring. "The big Greek guy that I was going to fight walked in and called my name while looking around to see who his opponent was going to be. 'Yeah, that's me,' I said, looking him straight in the eyes," Brendan said. "He looked around again and laughed. 'You?' He pointed to me, then looked at his coach. 'This guy?' 'Yeah, *me*!' I said. His coaches were laughing while talking in Greek; then I started to get really confident inside and said to my friend, 'I'm gonna get this guy!'"

So they walked out and entered the cage to start the battle. "This guy was round and a lot bigger than me, so he pushed me against the fence. I got stuck for a few seconds, but I got in a few shots, and we had a good ending to the first round," Brendan said. "I could see he was scared. I went to my corner, where my friend, who knows nothing about fighting, says, 'Good round!' The referee, who was also my opponent's coach, came over, looked me up and down, and said, 'No. We only do two rounds instead of three.' He probably could see his guy was getting tired." Brendan's friend suggested the judges may not let him win, so he'd better go for the knockout. "The bell sounded. I went at this guy—bomb, boom, boom, kick, boom, kick—and down he went!" Brendan said. "Manos Skoulas was his name, and I'll never forget. I got two hundred euros and a pair of gloves—that was it. I just fought my heart out. It was risky, but I didn't care," he said, beaming from ear to ear and laughing. He called his coach, Tony Mousah, after the fight. "Guess what? I have two wins as a professional now. I just won a fight in Greece. I had the opportunity, so I did it!"

Yet that aggressive fighting style was not part of his childhood growing up in the Manchester suburb of Fallowfield, where he enjoyed what he called an "average upbringing," running around outdoors, climbing trees, and playing soccer. Though he said he wasn't a great student, he did do well with history and still finds great enjoyment going to museums wherever he travels. Brendan was a natural athlete who participated in track and gymnastics as well as soccer during his early school years. "I had a knack for gymnastics and was one of the best in my school. I wish I would have pursued that, but I always leaned toward soccer. I wasn't very good at it but wanted to do it anyway," he said. "I remember staying in my garden for hours deep into the night, playing with my soccer ball. I was so hungry for anything that led to success and always worked hard." Eventually Brendan became captain of the local team at his school and even played at the semiprofessional level into high school, but he said it didn't take off for him because there was so much competition in soccer-rich Manchester, home to two of the English Premier League's greatest professional teams.

*   *   *

As a young kid, Brendan first became interested in fighting by watching the *Rocky* films. He loved to imagine what it would be like to have everybody watching him beat up somebody inside a ring. "I have a funny picture on my phone of me as a little kid with big boxing gloves, making a punching pose—no formal training or anything close to it, as I had only played soccer at that time. I used to see the martial arts people going in and out of the building and think, 'I'd love to do that one day,' but it never happened as a kid," he said. His parents worked long hours, so it was difficult to get to a class or pay for that kind of training. But when the UFC started to become popular, his upstairs neighbor, Ben Walker, was a professional MMA fighter in England when few others in his country were participating in the growing sport. "I didn't really want to do fighting as a sport, but I looked up to him so much that I thought, 'I'll just do whatever he is doing,' and we talked about it," Brendan said. "One day, when walking home from school, he brought me to his car and said, 'You're coming to training!' That was eleven years ago, and I haven't looked back since."

During his first MMA training experience, he met and worked out with Kane Mousah and a coach named Danny Ram outside in a park. "Danny said that ninety-nine percent of the people who train in MMA don't carry on. I've seen that many people come and go over the last ten years," Brendan said. "Some fighters do two or three years, and then they're gone because of injuries or starting families. There's so much that can get in the way of a professional fighting career," he said, shaking his head. Brendan believes anyone who can last a decade in an MMA career is exceptional, and he feels fortunate because the sport has more to offer than when he first started. "Now there are more financial opportunities and super training camps to focus on the depth of techniques in the sport."

Brendan is grateful for his training background in MMA, but he says kids should start off in gymnastics and go into other sports from there. "I don't recommend MMA to young kids; it's been a great personal journey, don't get me wrong. But it's made me do things like sacrifice my face and endure a lot of injuries, things I never would have dreamed of doing," he said, nodding. "I owe a lot to MMA, but I've missed social events and family time—finding a real girlfriend and keeping a stable relationship was difficult. It takes a special person to persevere through the ups and downs required in MMA."

After training a short time together in MMA, Brendan and Kane quickly moved to a new level in coaching excellence through

Kane's uncle, Tony Mousah, who coached Brendan forward into his amateur and professional career. "I have a very deep connection that developed with Tony after training for some time with Kane," said Brendan. "One time I fought on Saturday and Kane fought Sunday; then we went out partying. But by Tuesday I couldn't get in touch with him; by Wednesday I found out he had been arrested," he said. Kane was sentenced to ten years in prison for carrying firearms, a major offense in England versus the United States, where carrying a weapon is more prevalent and permitted by law. Since Brendan had started training with Tony only one month earlier, they wondered if they should carry on working together as a team. "Tony said, 'I'd love to teach ya,' so we have continued in that role since then, and he's been in my corner every fight."

Tony has been instrumental to Brendan's longevity in MMA, since it seemed to Brendan that, at times, Tony wanted success for him as a fighter more than he did. "It would be pouring down rain while we were training out in the park of Manchester, and even when it was snowing, he kept encouraging me to press on," Brendan said. "I have a deep loyalty to him as my coach, and I feel like we started this together, and we will end it together regardless of how much he thinks it might hold me back."

"It's been a bit of a crazy journey for me and Tony," Brendan said. He went 7–0 as an amateur and then 4–0 as a professional before driving to London for *The Ultimate Fighter* trials. Over three hours passed as he waited for the other auditioning competitors to fight, but only eight were going to be selected for the show. "I remember it getting down to the last fifty, twenty-five, then twelve, and I thought,

'Oh my gosh, I might have a chance here," he said. "But they got down to the very last ten and said, 'Go away, and we'll call you in three weeks.' They did call me and said, 'We want to let you know you haven't made the list. You are on the second reserve, but it has never been on the show. Keep fighting in England, and hopefully we'll see you again.' I was frustrated and said, 'How come I didn't even get an interview—I don't understand this. It doesn't make sense to me.' I *knew* I was supposed to be on that show!"

Brendan had a weird feeling about the whole situation, but he took a holiday in Spain a week later to relax and continue partying with his friends. The day he got back, he got a call from the UFC. "They told me, 'Just to let you know, one of the guys has been injured, so we need you to fly out tomorrow morning.' I thought, 'Whoa! The show was in Australia—twenty-four hours away!'" Brendan said. The show was the second foreign version of the UFC reality television series *The Ultimate Fighter*, with thirteen episodes filmed in Australia. "I sincerely considered not doing it, because I had just taken two weeks off partying and thought, 'You know you're not ready.' I had all these doubts in my head, but I did it anyway because this program was *'The Ultimate Fighter: The Smashes*, UK versus Australia, 2012,' and Ross Pearson was the coach," he said. Ross was the person who chose Brendan to be on his team for the show. "I got there straightaway and just *destroyed* Patrick Iodice by unanimous decision. I won the fight!"

*"It would be pouring down rain while
we were training out in the park of
Manchester, and even when it was snowing,
he kept encouraging me to press on."*

In the end, Brendan did not win the finale, but his appearance on the show, coming at a moment's notice, was certainly a huge leap ahead. "I kept thinking, 'I've come this far. I get headaches and injuries. But I'm in deep now, and this is what I want to fight for in my life, so I need to just keep moving forward,'" he said. Brendan fought his way through five more wins to earn the chance to compete for the world title on September 19, 2015, in the British Association of Mixed Martial Arts (BAMMA 22) but lost by a controversial split decision. "I was heartbroken, but the four hundred-plus messages I got from people in my local area were an inspiration to me," Brendan said. "I looked at all the support I had, and if it wasn't for them, I wouldn't be here. It's not just me on this journey. I said to myself, 'All right, Brendan, no matter what you want to do, you *have* to carry on—you have to show them you can do this.'"

Brendan has started participating in social media to begin reaching out to his fan base and interact with other fighters and sponsors to promote upcoming events. "Calling out people and talking crap online is something we have to do now, but I hate it— every second of it," he said. "It's the stupid part of the sport, and I believe the purest of martial artists and fans don't want to watch two fighters going at it, talking crazy to each other." Yet he's amazed at how hundreds of thousands of social media followers will watch an event on TV or at the arena as a result of the crazy talk, even if the fighters have not had many bouts. "I'm a martial artist. I want to shake your hand after we fight. I don't want to talk any crap beforehand. I just want to fight. Regardless of what happens, I will give you respect because I'm passionate about what I do, and I train my ass off—so I know that if you beat *me*, you must be very good because *you* just put your heart and soul into it too!"

> *"I'm a martial artist. I want to shake your hand after we fight. I don't want to talk any crap beforehand. I just want to fight."*

*   *   *

Brendan grew up in England, and indeed he is a popular athlete there, but he struggles with fame because he's always been a quiet person and said he didn't want to be "out there" in the fast-paced world. "It's one reason I like coming to the US, because I can just be on play mode and not have to speak to anyone," Brendan admitted. "Fake people try to call me to be my friend. But they aren't really my friend. What if I wasn't a fighter? Would he still be there? I shouldn't think like that, but I do."

Brendan believes it's probably even more difficult to be a high-level professional athlete or musician because it is difficult to discern whether people are real. "I have a friend who is a very famous rapper in England, and he's in the same boat I am. He doesn't leave his house anymore, because he doesn't trust anyone," Brendan said. "He wrote and produced a song about me because he said I inspired him. When he asked me if I wanted to hear it, I said no. It felt so crazy that he wrote about me, and *this* guy's a genius. I told him, 'I'll listen to it when it comes on the radio.' One day I'm driving and it comes on the radio—I couldn't believe it! After nine months of waiting, with it already on the charts and a pretty famous song in England, he really wanted me to hear it with him, so he took me to his car to play it." The song is called "Make or Break" by Bugzy Malone. "As fighters, we perfect our craft every day, but he does the same thing—it made an impact on me because of his ability to put his feelings into the words of a song that is so powerful, reaching others with the description of my life and this sport."

Since 2011, Brendan has been volunteering while perfecting his craft of MMA. He trains with the Phuket Top Team in Thailand and remembers being in that country one December to train with other competitors for an upcoming fight. "I woke up Christmas Day thinking, 'What can I do today that's gonna benefit me and others?' I started Googling 'orphanages in Thailand,' and there was one not too far from me. I told some of my friends that I was going, so they joined me too," Brendan said. "It was a very emotional experience. There were Christmas trees and gifts for these kids who were so poor, but they were super happy we were there! It touched my heart so deeply that I've been going there twice a year ever since, bringing gifts, toys, and playing soccer with them. The kids I met in the past are now all grown up, and they remember me. All these kids just need my time and to know they are loved."

Brendan also started a gym in 2013 called the All Powers Gym. It is located in England, and at the time it provided a place for troubled kids and street people to work out for free and receive

MMA training. Later, those same people had the opportunity to become trainers themselves. "It's crazy! I opened that gym, built it on goodwill, and held it together for four years. I never made any money but did it to help raise up the community and bring people off the streets," Brendan said. "We mentored them; the street people were run down and had no respect, but even so, I really connected with them. It was similar to what happened with me when my coach took me off the street and gave me what I needed, so I wanted to give back to other people."

But Brendan said some of those who he helped didn't feel loyal to him and were not as appreciative as he thought they would be. "When I told my organization partner, Panicos Yusuf, 'I have to take a step back because I'm so busy with fights at a higher level now, I can't continue to do all this training by myself,' he understood my decision very well. But when another fighter came in to take a leadership position, they all chose to begin charging everyone fees to participate. I was surprised by the response of a few guys I brought into the gym and trained up from the beginning who were now saying to me, 'I can't do it for free anymore,' even though I kept them together volunteering in these people's lives for so long," Brendan said, shaking his head in disbelief. "I learned a huge lesson. I won't be doing stuff for free anymore in that kind of a large scale, because I felt some strong resentment from some of them for moving on with my career. It was an unexpected twist that was ludicrous to me. Some people just don't appreciate my kind of dedication, but I'm grateful Panicos understands me as my good friend, and I continue to train there with my coach."

*   *   *

Among the misconceptions Brendan has heard about MMA, he has massive disdain for the idea that fighters are barbaric. "That really bothers me a lot because the dedication and hard work that it takes to get to this level is more than the majority of people could ever imagine. What we have to do and go through to stay ready in training is unachievable by most," he said. While those who are around the sport, such as siblings of fighters and coaches, understand the intensity required to be successful in MMA, Brendan believes others who sit back and watch the sport on TV need to understand that fighters are not animals. "You can't really blame them when they see blood spit everywhere, but at the same time I want to get across to people that I've got much of my life invested in this profession, and it takes great skill," he said. "I have a friend who is a construction worker, and he said he wished he had my life because he thought it was easy. I said, 'Come train with me for just one day.' He did one three-hour session, then told me, 'You do this three times a day, man? I'm *amazed*! I take back everything I said."

"This is my passion. It's what I was born to do. It doesn't feel like work to me," Brendan added, resting between workouts at San Diego's Alliance Gym. "Right now I'm just thinking about training again tomorrow and how great it's going to be. Dominick Cruz, who has been a massive inspiration to me, did some great sparring with me today! I just love it. It's a deep desire that lights my fire, keeps me alive, and motivates me to be better all the time."

Brendan first met Dominick after he was called in from the

second reserve to participate in *The Ultimate Fighter* in Australia. While filming the show, Brendan also experienced an instant connection with Jimmy Harbison, the jiu-jitsu coach for Ross's team, because of their shared Irish heritage. Jimmy stayed in England with Brendan for a while after that and then invited Brendan to come to San Diego and train with Dominick at Alliance to prepare for Brendan's first fight with Tanko.

> *"What we have to do and go through to stay ready in training is unachievable by most."*

"Since I had never left England before and never trained in the US, I knew I should go to Alliance, one of the top MMA gyms in the nation, and train for my big fight. Jimmy then asked me, 'Do you want to come and live with Dominick? He has an extra bedroom there, and you could stay there while you train.' I thought that was crazy! What an opportunity!" Brendan got to San Diego as quickly as he could, arriving at night after a long series of flights. Jimmy picked him up at the airport and took him to the house. "In the morning Dominick popped his head in and said to me, 'Hey, man! Anything you need while you're here, just let me know.' I yawned and asked him, 'How did this work out so good?' Dom responded, 'Jimmy knows what I'm like. He never brings anyone around me that he knows is not right.' I was so amazed and taken aback," Brendan said with admiration.

"Ever since then it's been a beautiful connection. Even if my fighting ended tomorrow, I'd stay friends with Jimmy and

Dominick," Brendan added. "I owe everything to MMA; it has brought me to all parts of the world and introduced me to people I would never have met—some of the best people in my life."

Family has been a strong advantage for Brendan. Though he is an only child, he is close with his cousins and grandparents. His parents separated about five years ago because they had grown apart. "That's fine. People grow old and separate," Brendan said. "My dad didn't come to my fights or soccer games as a kid. I don't resent him or anything, and he still came to visit me, but now he has started coming to watch my fights. I'm working on a better connection with him." It was Brendan's mother, Agnes Conneely, who paid for things, drove him to training, and handled everything for him, supporting her son even though she never came to his fights early in his career.

"I said no years ago because she means so much to me, and if I take a beating, I didn't want her to see that. I was afraid I would get hurt in front of her," Brendan admitted. "Recently, though, I realized I'm getting older, and so is she. All her friends go to the fights, and she gets nervous—everyone else in the world gets to see me compete, but she doesn't. So I had a fight that I was confident about and finally asked her if she wanted to go. She said, 'I've always wanted to come, but it's your decision.' I said, 'I want you to come to one fight.' Now she's addicted and won't miss any of them!" he said, laughing. "I know that I'm at a different level now, and I might be injured, but I don't get hurt that bad. I'm glad she's there."

At the start of his career, Brendan kept a diary. "I wrote, 'Your mom had three jobs to keep you in this. Don't quit!' Another entry said, 'Your mom worked hard to get you where you are today!' She paid for sessions when we weren't well off and toughed it out with expensive things like training gear and gym fees," he said. "Mom also gave me a cross that she was given by my grandmother when she was twenty-one. I wear it all the time when I'm not fighting because it's my good luck charm, as if my mom is with me everywhere I go." He said she always supported him, cooking his meals right and telling him, "Do what you want to do. I'll support you regardless." Brendan said, "I always wanted to be successful and give back to her the way she gave to me. That's why I'm so dedicated, and I don't miss a session, because it's a full-time job. I'm blessed with what I do and take it very seriously."

> "I owe everything to MMA; it has brought
> me to all parts of the world and
> introduced me to people I would never
> have met—some of the best people
> in my life."

Brendan believes he's had a good life and doesn't want to complain about anything because he has come so far since beginning his career in 2008. The back-and-forth brawls, with wins and split decisions that took place in multiple arenas throughout the UK, have given him great experience to continue moving forward. "The disheartening feeling of recent judge's decisions that didn't go my way made me look up at the mountain from the bottom again," Brendan said. "I thought, 'I really don't want to start this journey again.' But I'm still young and lucky to enjoy training, or I don't know how much longer I could stand it."

Currently with Absolute Championship Berkut, Brendan closed 2017 with a huge win over Paata Tschapelia, who had never before lost by knockout. During the fight, Brendan broke his forearm in the second round, when he landed a devastating spinning backhand fist to the head of his contender. He pushed through the pain to deliver a knee to the back of the ribcage and then a precise head kick to finish off Tschapelia in the final minute of the third round. Brendan hopes the result will allow him to fulfill his desire to be part of the UFC because he feels he is definitely in the same category talent wise as their fighters.

"I fought with titles in two different weights, while other guys are getting signed with far less success and experience. Am I doing something to piss these guys off? I don't understand why. I'm exciting, jumping up with strong kicks and putting on good, hard, entertaining fights. But at the same time I've gotten back to my roots. I left the gym, left my house because I travel so much, and moved home to my mom because she's done everything for me and my dreams. In the long term, it will be best for everybody. That's how my team is looking at this reality. I love the training—really enjoy the fight and the lifestyle—but I can't wait for that next defining moment, because I'm always battle ready!"

Handwritten inscription: thank you uncle James hope you enjoy my story, I means the world to me

5

Danny Martinez
TOUGH LITTLE WARRIOR WITH A BIG HEART

Handwritten signature: The GREMLIN

The UFC 193 event in Australia on November 14, 2015, made history as the most viewed pay-per-view event to that time and is best known for Ronda Rousey's bantamweight title defeat to Holly Holm. Yet, digging deeper into the card, there is an amazing story of professional and personal victory to be told about Danny "the Gremlin" Martinez. The flyweight fighter from Tempe, Arizona, scored big when he defeated Richie Vaculik via unanimous decision (30–27, 30–27, 30–27) for his first-ever win in the UFC organization. More than that, it became a serious game changer in his career and life, as he flipped a significant mental switch in preparation for the bout.

"The only thing I feared was loss of breath from lack of conditioning," he said, "but I totally overcame that in the last camp." A fit, multidimensional fighter who had compiled a strong 18–7 record in prior matches, Danny nevertheless found himself plagued with fear in his mind as UFC 193 neared. "That's why I went with George Castro as my strength and conditioning coach, because head coach Eric Del Fierro and I knew the way I fight—gritty, rough—just get in there and throw hands in a dirty fight. I had to be so conditioned that I didn't have any hesitation thinking I would blow my lungs out, gas out, or lose the battle, which happened in the Scott Jorgenson fight. I was stuck in the middle of the third round and couldn't even hold my hands up, and he just kept punching."

His anxiety was so extreme that images of his failure invaded his dreams at night. It was a gripping reality that caused Danny to alter his mental approach so that he could be ready to block the punches and continue to blow through the walls of his lung capacity to gain every inch. "That's exactly what I did three times a week with George. It was ridiculous! Treadmill sprints at eleven incline and ten speed for one minute and then fifteen minutes with a spotter holding me at the waist so I don't fall. I was just killing it!" Danny said. "The fact is, I told my brain before the fight, 'This is what you gotta do; this is it!' George said to me, 'Every workout you do, you gotta hate it and have a visual situation because it's the only way you're gonna give up the thought that you're gonna lose. You can't gas out, but think instead, 'I gotta run; I gotta hold my hands up.'"

Danny flipped the switch with just eight weeks to go before the Vaculik fight and told his body that it was working for this fight every second. "Once I started doing that," he said, smiling, "all those workouts for the next six weeks were constant killers, consistently telling my brain, 'Let's do this.' I just stopped getting tired and got conditioned instead; my mind was better. My confidence level two weeks before the fight was so different. I was walking around before our sparring sessions, laughing and joking. The team would say, 'Danny, what are you doing?' I'd say, 'I'm ready, dog! I'm not going to get tired.'"

If the biggest fear of sparring is getting tired, then being a wrestler—a "prepared to grind fighter"—was also key to getting it done, and Danny's wrestling experience in high school and college, training from mat greats like Efrain Escudero, Jamie Varner, and Anthony Birchak, served him well. He knew he wasn't going to get weary, because he could let his hands go and wrestle when needed. "Since my wrestling looked so good, my mind was just triggered to say, 'You can do whatever you want.' Some people hold back, but wrestlers go for fifteen minutes; they know how hard it is. That was everything that conditioned my brain and won the fight!"

UFC 193 was also a big payday for Danny, but he said he really didn't care about that. Instead, he looks forward to competing with himself and focusing on honing his ability to keep entering the octagon. While his twenty-one wins going into summer 2017 were fewer than he desired, he continued building up his confidence, priding himself on being ready to accept a challenge fight on a moment's notice. "I won the UFC 193 fight, which was a stepping block into the UFC with the biggest attendance in history. Then I took the Combates Americas fight on ten days' notice and had to cut twenty-five pounds. It was another win by decision, and these were certainly the steps in the right direction for my career."

For years Danny thought that being mentally strong was more

about just running all the time without listening to his mind, but now he is quickly learning that "… having a hammer-strong mind is about controlling yourself, noticing that if you're going all over the place with your actions or emotions outside the cage, you need to bring it back to the fight life real fast before it's too late. Learning to control my mind is what I'm working on the most."

His next fight after Combates Americas was with the Absolute Championship Berkut, his third different organization in consecutive fights. This time he had only an eight-week notice to get ready for an opponent who was a military vet with a winning record. Danny said that early 2017 bout helped him learn to control his mind *inside* the fight—not just going after it and winging the punches and kicks but thinking about what he wanted to do. "Sometimes you need to believe you can control the fight like a chess match, protecting your position so you don't get hurt, and I had to learn that to further my career," Danny said. "During this three-fight win streak, I had a position of power in the fight game, with three wins in different organizations. I felt like I could hold my hand and cards up high and let everybody know, 'Hey, I'm Danny Martinez, and I can fight. I've got everything under control."

*   *   *

It wasn't always that way for Danny Martinez, and like many who overcome tragedy in their lives, his appreciation for the support of his family through difficult situations led him into his successful fighting career. Growing up as a kid in Tempe, Danny became interested in wrestling at the age of nine by watching his older brother,

Chris, at middle school wrestling practice. Danny saw guys on the mat throwing each other around and figured out martial arts right away because kicking and punching was "the thing to do" with his twin brother, Jo Jo, in the living room at home. Danny started wrestling daily in sixth grade in addition to playing football. "Wrestling as the smallest and the strongest kid made me feel like I was the strongest little one out of all of them." The following year Danny placed fourth in the city; over the next five years, his middle school team won two city titles, and his high school earned two state titles, at one point ranking in the top twenty nationally.

Every week in high school, he had to cut weight from his usual 130 pounds down to 119 to be eligible to compete. "I didn't really know how to cut weight, so I just stopped eating for three days to make weight. It was a tough junior and senior year," he said. "I had bad grades and sometimes ditched school, but some of the teachers worked with me and let me leave class to train and cut weight because the team was so good."

"Wrestling as the smallest and the strongest kid made me feel like I was the strongest little one out of all of them."

Danny's mother attended his wrestling tournaments throughout high school. "My mom was always there and wanted to give me a hug and kiss. She was proud of me, and my dad sometimes gave me encouraging words. But one time, at the end of my junior year, he was preparing to go to jail for a short time. He sat me down and told me, 'You have a wrestling heart, and the stuff I'm telling you is serious. It's gonna help me get through this time, seeing you do so well,'" Danny said. "I had the summer to get even better, and he let me know I was giving him hope. He wasn't worried, because I was going to be okay. He had trust in me. It was a compliment to me. He had never acted like that before." Danny's solemn expression then gave way to laughter. "I'm not the one to give a pat on the back to. Out of all four of us kids, he paid more money for me because I was the only one who had traffic tickets!"

His parents also gave him confidence to continue wrestling beyond high school, even after he wasn't offered a college scholarship like many of his teammates. "After graduating high school in 2003, they reassured me of this great opportunity to go forward to Pima Community College in Tucson. They helped me find a place to stay, and after I moved out there bought me groceries and supported me as I wrestled for two years," Danny said. He added that it was great building the beginning of his fighting career at Pima while talking to his parents every day on the phone. It was also at Pima where his interest in MMA sparked as he trained with teammates Varner, Escudero, and Birchak, along with Drew Ficket and Jessy Forbes.

It was late 2005 when Danny made the decision to drop out of college and become involved in MMA as a professional fighter. But it was also then, when in his early twenties, that he had two close friends lose their lives in freak accidents. The first friend lost was Enrique "Chito" Sanchez. He was like a brother to Danny, a kindhearted guy beloved in their neighborhood who played with little kids and always paid attention to Danny. "I remember going to his house every day, and even though I bothered him, he always had time for kids that were younger than him." When Danny was twenty-one, Chito was killed in a DUI accident. "A guy asked Chito if he and a friend wanted a ride just up the road to a tournament, so they jumped into the back of the truck. The man was drunk and hit a dirt lip going eighty, smashed into the curb, and flipped the truck. Three people died, two people lived; the driver survived and one of Chito's cousins too."

The other friend, Big Gilbert Aldana, was a UFC heavyweight fighter who met Danny daily to train, along with welterweight Seth Baczynski. Danny said Seth and Gilbert did the hard training but always made sure he got in there as a twenty-year-old, 140-pound kid who didn't know anything. Though he was never sure if they actually wanted him there, Danny always showed up to work out at 5:00 a.m. Just like Chito, they gave up their time for him. Gilbert coached Danny, telling him, "You gotta live, get in, and get out of this sport, because it's all about getting what you want in this game. Save the pennies, and get free training as much as you can without spending the money or time to travel. Move into a gym, and sleep on people's couches to save money. Do what you want to achieve, then get out and support your family and have a good time." Gilbert died in a boating accident after jumping into the water to grab a T-shirt. The water was too cold and put his body into shock, making it impossible to move his hands or limbs," Danny said. "He was a heavyweight and could not swim out, so he sank down into the water and drowned."

For the next five years following those tragedies, Danny's life slid into turmoil, spiraling downward into the depths of depression, alcoholism, and bad decisions between professional fights because of the deeply hurtful loss of his friends and mentors. The troublemaking snowball effect disintegrated all his family relationships and career choices.

"Being on my own after dropping out of college, moving back to Phoenix, training for my MMA career, and trying to make rent just took a toll on me," Danny said. "The way I acted while choosing a job to work late in bars and getting out at four a.m., what else am I going to do at that time in the morning? People asked me to come over and drink until ten a.m., and there was nothing else to think about that was good, so I drank very heavily. That was a big issue for me." It got so bad, Danny said, that when he wasn't fighting or training for a camp, he was sitting in the prison cell or the drunk tank three times a week. "One of my family members had to come pick me up, or I would get dropped off at their house at six a.m."

But then Danny experienced an amazing breakthrough that not only changed his life but reignited his fighting career. Seth Baczynski, Danny's longtime training partner, was friends with Dominick Cruz, who was training in California for the WEC bantamweight title against Brian Bowles. Seth knew Danny's fight game was a good match for Dominick to practice drills during training. "They got together and brought me out to California for the whole camp. I dropped everything and went there for two weeks," Danny said. "I got a release from the court to travel to San Diego, and I made the best of it because I knew the timing was important. We went to Big Bear Lake, and I remember the first Monday practice I had to do sprints with Dominick at five in the morning. It was crazy! The sun wasn't even up yet, and I asked, 'What day is it?' He would wake me up early to help him train every day, twice a day. I'd never had that level of commitment in my training over the previous six years of my career!"

When he returned to Phoenix after Dominick won the title at WEC 47 on March 6, 2010, Danny knew that he had to get back to San Diego and advance his own career. He quickly got in touch with his probation officer and made his case for moving to California for this important opportunity. The officer told the judge on their court date that Danny would have five fights supporting Dominick in training, and that he'd be making good money teaching kid's classes at the Alliance Gym at the same time. They also gave the judge a note from Coach Eric stating that Danny was doing well. "The judge said, 'If this is true, and you can leave Arizona today, I'd be happy to take you off of probation,'" Danny said, grinning. "So I gathered everything, said goodbye to my family, and was ready to go with Dominick, who was fighting Joseph Benavidez again to defend his title."

Teaching kids was something new for Danny, and he quickly gave his whole heart to his students while the families made him feel loved, inviting him to birthday parties and celebrations. He met new people, discovered exciting levels of personal success, and was grateful, as Alliance took care of him by providing a job and a place to stay for the next three years. Danny found it all to be a different grind than wrestling; teaching martial arts full-time while training twice a day as a fighter was rough. "I was there for the love of it, knowing I was still moving forward," he said. "I took those kids to tournaments because that's where they learn about character. We built the team foundation, choosing our captains who were loyal members, and created a positive team atmosphere for competition. "They learned it's not just about going to classes or getting stripes and belts for attendance; it's about achieving something great into their future."

> *"They learned it's not just about going to classes or getting stripes and belts for attendance; it's about achieving something great into their future."*

*   *   *

Danny met Kellie Ventre at a WEC championship fight in Arizona for Dominick Cruz against Scott Jorgenson in 2010. He spent time at the fight with the tall brunette real estate agent from Phoenix, and they later talked over the phone and made occasional trips to meet in Yuma—between Phoenix and San Diego—to see Bellator fights. "We were just going to be friends," Kellie said, "but Danny is such a genuine, good person that one thing led to another."

When he first got to San Diego, Danny said he lived like a soldier in close quarters at the gym because he was told that he should keep personal relationships completely separated from his fighting. As coach Gilbert had said, "move into a gym, and sleep on people's couches to save money." Danny and Kellie dated, and she was supportive of his teaching and training, but the long-distance aspect of their relationship was difficult, as was his sincere belief about strict dedication to his profession. After about three months, they broke up, but only briefly. Kellie knew she cared deeply for Danny, so she made a big career move to San Diego in 2011 for a new opportunity in real estate and to be closer to Danny. While he still lived at the gym, she bought a house, and the couple worked on solidifying their relationship, which was a plus for Danny. Kellie supported him in his career, and he won the next four fights in a row. During this time Kellie became pregnant with their daughter. "I moved in with Kellie a month before we had our first daughter, Esmee, in October of that year," Danny said, "but before that, it felt like I was part of two teams: the team of brotherhood and then the team at home. I was mixed up on it for a while, but things began to change for the better when I finally moved from the gym to share a home with Kellie and our daughter."

That sense of separation was exasperated by Danny's insistence that Kellie not attend any of his fights, stemming from what he had been told and therefore believed about separation of his personal existence from his professional one. "At first he didn't even want me talking about it or being with him at anything," she said. "It was hard for me because I wasn't allowed to be part of the gym. It was really tricky until he finally stopped listening to everyone else and moved here with me. Then things got better, but it took about two years. Now he tells me everything—how he's feeling with his workouts and training. I'm part of his team now."

"I had her off on a little island," Danny admitted, "and I had to learn how to sacrifice myself as a fighter but not to leave my family behind so I could work hard on my dreams. I discovered how to give my family their time, then go back and give at the gym to get the coaching I needed."

While Danny always knew he wanted to win the UFC flyweight championship, he eventually realized his work with the kids at Alliance was becoming a distraction from that goal. "I loved teaching and being that person to those kids, but I also lost the picture of the belt instilled in my mind for years, so I had to quit teaching the kids' classes in 2013. I went back to training full-time." From that point forward, a little more than two years passed before Danny's pivotal UFC 193 fight in Australia. In that same time, his relationship with Kellie deepened, particularly during the camp leading up to that event. By then their second daughter, Lula, had been born. Kellie was doing great in her real estate career, and Danny was progressing as a fighter. After training hard twice a day, he felt loved going home every day to his family. But there was one thing left undone.

"I had to learn how to sacrifice myself as a fighter but not to leave my family behind so I could work hard on my dreams. I discovered how to give my family their time, then go back and give at the gym to get the coaching I needed."

"We still weren't married," Kellie said, "but one time Esmee called me 'Mommy Martinez' out of nowhere. It took having our second daughter to get us thinking about marriage, and I didn't expect it, either, because I had been married before."

One day Danny was playing with Esmee and admiring his little daughter when he spoke to her in an endearing voice and asked, "Esmee, will you marry me?" She declared, "You should marry Mommy!" Danny said, "It hit me hard in the head. 'Why *aren't* we married?'" The next day Danny proposed, and he and Kellie agreed to be wed in secret because he was concerned his coaches might be against him getting married. It was seven in the morning when they were wed by a justice of the peace in El Cajon. "We have the best wedding picture!" Danny said, laughing. Kellie giggled and added, "No, it was amazingly horrible. Esmee was tired, Lula was sick, and it was so funny."

That same morning Danny went to his final sparring session before departing for Australia. Coach Eric said, "Dang, Danny, you look good! You look good!" Danny was saying to himself, "Hee-hee! That's because I just got married!" Later, Danny learned that Eric actually laughed when he saw a Facebook post about the marriage that same afternoon.

Now that he was married, Danny focused more on his relationship with Kellie and his girls, finding inspiration from his own parents. "Dad put my mom first, even over his friends. He'd stay home if my mom had to work; he always put the family first," Danny said. "I told myself, 'You moved here, you had your family here, you wanted to be at this gym. You can't feel bad because you have your kids and family now; you just have to work twice as hard.'" Being married also made a significant difference because he said it broke the chains of people telling him earlier in his career that he and his family life would have to be separate. "Even though she still doesn't come to the fights, I tell her exactly how I'm feeling during the weight cut or any other details in the days leading up to a fight. We text and communicate," he said, adding that the fight game's uncontrolled environment is why he remained concerned with Kellie attending fights. "MMA events are far more furious than other sporting events, with people yelling at each other. It's important to me that she doesn't go through that."

At first Kellie didn't understand his view, and it even hurt her feelings. But she knows Danny feels strongly about it. "I personally think it's in his head, because I'm not the type of person that gets scared; plus, I've been to a bunch of other fights, but I don't need to go. I'm honoring his wishes. Now he needs that loving support of, 'I love you' or 'I miss you.'"

Because of this, Danny knows that Kellie is there for him. "She put in the work to be a big part of my life—the hard stuff to stay inside my life and career. I feel the gratitude and the emotional impact she's trying to present to me. That's the nice part about relationships that some men just don't understand—it's not about being separate but being together with one another to build up and encourage each other. Some people think that's the weak part, but I think being together shows love more than anything," Danny said. "She has been there from the very beginning, and hanging in there through all the challenges is probably the roughest part of being the spouse to a fighter in this sport."

Although their careers are very different, Danny and Kellie realize they share many things in common, such as the need to be self-motivated, determined, and consistent in going forward, because no one gets paid until they have completed the work.

"Neither of us brings home a check until the house sells or the fight is won," Kellie said. "It's really difficult sometimes." Then Danny bragged that Kellie closed on houses during three consecutive camps the final week before his fights. "We were literally doing the hot dog and ramen food thing for a month or two," Kellie said, "then he fights and I close on a house at the same time. We're always far behind, but we get to catch up for a month or two with bills being paid. We pray that another house will close. It's been tough."

"Yeah," Danny said, "it's still a lot of praying and timing over the last two years." It has also helped to have contracted fights with organizations such as UFC, Combate Americas, and Absolute Championship Berkut. Ongoing fight contracts are a significant need for a fighter to succeed in mixed martial arts and to provide for his or her family. Recently, Danny and Kellie were driving in their car with two high school boys getting ready for wrestling season. Danny had trained the boys years earlier. One of them asked, "Hey, Coach, how much money did you make in Australia?"

Behind the wheel, Danny glanced at the boys in his rearview mirror and then smiled and said to Kellie, "Oh God, here it comes!"

"Tell 'em!" Kellie said excitedly.

"No, I can't," Danny responded. "They don't understand money or making a dollar. I could tell them a big number, and they'd think, 'That's a lot!' But it's *not* a lot."

Kellie was persistent. "Tell them, because they need to know what they're looking forward to in their future."

He looked in the rearview mirror again, and both boys were looking at him with anticipation. "Okay. Let's say I show up for a fight, win, maybe get a bonus, and get fifty thousand dollars. A percentage of that goes to my team and my manager. Because it took place in Australia, another one third is removed in taxes. Then, after my expenses for food, hotel incidentals, and other travel needs are taken out, only seventy-five hundred is left. That's what I actually make."

Kellie turned in the passenger seat to face the two boys. "So, if Danny fights three times per year, and he's lucky, he can bring home about half of what a schoolteacher makes in a year."

"Their faces were priceless," Danny recalled. "They tried to justify it and make me feel better for my career misfortune." He laughed. "A lot of people want to have kids and a great house, but it's not likely in MMA. I told them to think about what they're doing. Living in the limelight is real, as is all that comes with it, and yes, they might have money. But it'll only be for a short window of time."

Danny believes that the amount of money MMA fighters make is misunderstood by the public, with most fans thinking there's as much money to be made in mixed martial arts as in other professional sports offering multimillion-dollar contracts. He said the reality is far different. When an amateur begins to fight professionally, for example, he or she is required to pay for the qualifying prefight medical tests, the license fees, and dental bills afterward, plus any other doctor appointments. There is no insurance available after each bout unless the fighter is in the UFC or another professional organization. "I can only go to the dentist right after my fight for dental work because my fillings get knocked out," Danny said.

At the end of each fight camp before a bout, Danny points out that he's usually broke. "I barely have money to go to the hotel to get incidentals like protein bars and electrolyte drinks before my fight. It's so hard because I don't want to overcharge my credit card. I always wanted to fight and did it while I was poor, living in the gym," he said, "but now I've got kids and a wife, so even though I have some income from sponsorships, I have to do this because I love it. There's no real money at the average levels for MMA athletes. I tell kids, 'Take an honest look at your future, because you can always do better making a life for yourself than MMA.'"

Even when a fighter becomes a champion, Danny said they only keep their earnings "for a few years, plus they have to give a lot back in luxury taxes." He says MMA fighters must live within their means. "… and most importantly, if they want kids, have kids. But they shouldn't run around in a Maserati if their children aren't taken care of. I was single, grew into fatherhood, and now I'm a married man. I'm now in a different ballpark."

*   *   *

While the fear he once had about conditioning is gone, Danny still gets anxious during the days after a match is over—but in a good way. He and all fighters must observe a mandated medical respite after each bout, but every morning at ten thirty he gets goosebumps because his mind and body tell him it's time to be back at Alliance with his team. Whether Danny is at home or elsewhere, he catches himself staring out the window, obsessing about training. The fact that he feels that rush of adrenaline at the same time each morning tells Danny that he has shifted his career mind-set to stay on top of his fight game.

In early 2017, Danny signed a four-fight contract with Fight Night Global to assure himself of well-paying fights for the next twelve months. Shooto, one of the oldest organizations from Japan, also contacted him about a fight with Hiromasa Ogikubo, one of the top contenders, who had fought three different champions in six weeks. Danny knew Ogikubo was a tough opponent, and the pay was less than he had received for a single fight since 2012, but he said the opportunity was worth it. "The money doesn't mean anything when the numbers are there. The ability to get back to where I want to be in my career at this time and place in my life, at age thirty-two, is like I'm sitting at a craps table at four in the morning, and my friend took all my chips to my room, saying, 'Okay, this is what you have left: a four-fight deal back in the room of the hotel.'" The fight with Ogikubo went to a judges' decision, and his opponent won, but Danny felt great about it. "I went out there to focus on the fight and have fun like I was going to Disneyland—confident, like I was going to show off a new suit," he said. "I trained hard like I wanted to, and I was huge and looked strong—even the commentators talked about our size difference." He also said he discovered a culture of peace in Japan. He was treated with respect as a great fighter; they appreciated him being there, and they wanted him to come back.

Danny loves to stay busy and focused on his fighting career, but he is looking ahead at his future in a sport where everyone wants to retire, but no one wants to retire too young because it's like giving up on their dream. He said, "There are great athletes in the sport that say, 'It's not time to walk away when you *think* it's your time to walk away from the sport, but when they *make* you walk away.' I'm in the life of fighting because I chose this career, and as long as my body is healthy and giving me what I want at the highest level to compete, then I have to honor that."

There's a saying, however: don't work harder, work smarter. Danny applied this to his life when he began to focus on his fighting career. He still wanted to assist young kids, so before he stopped coaching youngsters at Alliance Gym, Danny started an organization in 2012 called Gremlin's Kids, emphasizing antibullying. "Working smarter was the key to my future, and to this day when we host a Gremlin's Kids event, it's scheduled *after* a fight with full camp because that needs to be my focus," Danny said. "I know that the fight is the fight, and that's why I'm here. It is my credibility as a professional fighter that attracted people to what I'm doing with Gremlin's Kids in our community." He and other fighters take students who have attended past Gremlin's Kids events and go to Boys and Girls Clubs and similar after-school programs to talk to students about the effects of bullying. He wants kids to create a good atmosphere at school and encourages them to show up to class. The fighters also share stories, reveal truths about bullying, and talk about when they were bullied by other kids.

"I share everything with them, even that I was a bully because of the way I came off against others but didn't know it," Danny said. He discusses how his brother used to get bullied but didn't tell anybody, so he'd go beat up the bully but end up being the one caught and suspended. Then, while he was stuck at home, his brother was still being bullied. "This could have been fixed if my brother would have told the teacher," Danny said. "It would have saved a lot of time." During a Gremlin's Kids event, Danny says the bullies themselves are sometimes right there in the room. "It makes them think about their actions. It evens out the odds, and often the entire room gets emotional when students cry in front of the whole class."

Many children who attend Gremlin's Kids report that they are no longer being bullied. "This one boy got kicked in his face, so we had a group talk about the situation. He didn't want to talk about it, but when other kids started sharing, they all got emotional. Everyone is nice to him now because he stood up, and they appreciated him doing that. They all shed some tears," Danny said. "You have to let the kids handle it without hiding things, or they don't know how to properly get through their emotions."

Danny says he feels like a kid again when he spends time with the high school students who have come through Gremlin's Kids and are now leaders reaching out to other students. He and Kellie will often go out to eat or hang out at their house with the older student leaders on Sunday to show how much he appreciates their support and help. In turn, they value his time and investment when he takes them to be part of the events.

He believes everyone should be giving and supporting others who are in need within the community, and it's not a just religious act to do so on Sunday. "Some people go to church. I'm not a religious man, but I say we need to worship humanity too," Danny said. "I'm not knocking anyone who's religious, but if you're going to worship someone, honor good humans as they walk with us." He tells these kids that they don't have to be religious to be good to people, and they seem to understand and respect what he's doing, and he admires them as well.

He often tells the student leaders, "You tell me what you need, and I got you." He gives them training gear that he's received for his sponsorships so they can benefit from it. He says they can't afford training gear, so they earn it—it's not welfare. He knows the value of working to earn things, so he has developed this part of Gremlin's Kids with that in mind. He also wants to help them succeed in life and accomplish what they want to do. "Their confidence level exceeds what I had at their age, and they know how to use it. One of the strongest keys we utilize in our program is having a kid build up someone else's confidence," Danny said. "It's good they know what I'm trying to do. Gremlin's Kids are going to continue to teach Gremlin's Kids into the future."

With a desire to reach out to others beyond the students through Gremlin's Kids, Danny decided to begin helping the homeless, which he understands from experience. His brother Chris opened his home to him years earlier after the tragic deaths of Chito and Gilbert, and Danny stayed with him for a year. Today Danny is uncle to Chris's two little kids. Back when Danny was struggling with depression, his sister, Drea, and her two small boys helped him through it. Now they are nine and ten, and Danny teaches them wrestling. When his twin brother, Jo Jo, became a heroin addict, Danny used a bonus from a fight to pay for an addiction program, and he's drug free today. "My brothers are my loudest fans. My sister moved here, and now my parents are moving here after they sell their home in Arizona so we can all be together. They are all an inspiration to me."

Danny and Kellie first turned that inspiration into service in 2014 by cooking up donated carne asada, beans, and rice to serve to the homeless and fans hanging out outside San Diego Chargers football games. They watched TV and tailgated, and some came with blankets and sleeping bags so they could get donated clothing and eat some good food. After a while, though, the gatherings became rowdy and potentially unsafe, so someone recommended they go to Father Joe's Villages. It's a large nonprofit community organization in San Diego that offers multiple transitional home and care programs for the homeless. It serves approximately 2,900 veterans per year, supports more than 780 children, and houses more than 1,800 people every day.

Danny got involved with Father Joe's Villages because he felt better about serving those trying to do something with their lives versus people intentionally staying out on the street. He believes they're in a tough situation because they could have a drug addiction or have been unexpectedly struck homeless when they had a bad week of work, got fired, and were then unable to pay their bills and lost their homes. "In my MMA world, bills get stacked up before I get a paycheck, but I can count on those funds eventually being there for me. But if you're homeless, money doesn't come, and there's no one to help if you're on the street. They didn't plan for that to happen," he said. "People shouldn't shame the homeless.

The level of difficulty to get out of the homeless life—it's a hard way to climb."

For his first Thanksgiving serving at Father Joe's, Danny had custom fight shirts made to raise money to purchase ninety turkeys and a three-course dinner, with salad, dessert, and all the fixings for nine hundred families. "Everyone had seconds," he said. "It was good to connect with them." Danny then helped the following month with a Christmas celebration that included photos with Santa, a hired deejay to play Christmas carols, and a special station where kids could make their own cards and gifts for their parents. Stocking stuffers and board games were given to 150 kids, and children under one received a blanket with a stuffed animal and pajamas donated by mothers of San Diego Chargers players.

Because of Danny's involvement, word of mouth snowballed and more people got involved, culminating Easter 2016 with kids making baskets and a special presentation honoring Danny with the Father Joe's Village Award. Tommy Lovell, a well-known concerned citizen and social justice warrior in San Diego, spoke at the event. "Danny is a professional MMA fighter who travels to elementary schools presenting his 'I Hate Bullies' anti-bullying program but also has engaged in fighting homelessness," Lovell said, "all while training relentlessly to be ready at any moment for an unscheduled opportunity to fight. In addition, he is a father and husband." Danny was grateful for and humbled by this recognition. "This award is for compassion. One time they acknowledged me in the UFC, saying I have a huge heart, initiative, and knockout power," Danny said. "I tell all my kids that no one can ever take my heart away when I retire. So we all have a heart, and we all have compassion in our heart whenever we breathe—so as long as you keep breathing, give that compassion to someone who needs it."

> *"I tell all my kids that no one can ever take my heart away when I retire. So we all have a heart, and we all have compassion in our heart whenever we breathe—so as long as you keep breathing, give that compassion to someone who needs it."*

Each year the events at Father Joe's expand, and the kids now bring their own tables and supply their own gifts to give out to others. "It's cool because there's much more to this than kids getting socks and gifts," Kellie said. "These things happen because Danny brings so many people with him to serve everyone with cheer. We don't know many people with a lot of money, but it's the whole community—including families that have trained with Danny, Gremlin's Kids, and others—that are coming together with their meal that they made to give away or with their one turkey to donate. They're little parts that now make up the big one. They're our number one support, and frequently the new kids at Father Joe's ask if they can come to help us in community service."

Danny thinks that anyone who chooses to donate to Father Joe's will see the obvious need. "Many of these families have four or five kids, with some of them disabled. They have nothing, but I give everything I can," Danny said. "We have two healthy kids, our home, and we get to be together; it's all we want. Our girls are wonderful and all the entertainment we need!" Danny laughed. "But this didn't just happen overnight; it took a while. I didn't notice it right away either. It took me some time to realize it's going to be okay. If my parents can do this life together, so can we."

Finally, Danny wants everyone to see that if they know a troubled or even bothersome kid or grown up, they should find time to play with that child or help that adult, because you never know what you might do to change their life so they will impact others. "Helping your city and being in a position to give back is priceless because these opportunities are given to you. You may lead another generation to the same purpose I have found, and they might make it out to be safe from a troubled life," Danny said. "I have to thank Chito and Big Gilbert for showing me how to reach out to others. I always talk to those two before my fights. They left a big impact on my life, and they are still here with me. They've seen my whole career from heaven."

Thom Ortiz

*COACHING OTHERS TO SUCCESS,
LIVING HIS DREAM*

Thom Ortiz's life has been a mix of heart-soaring success and heart-wrenching tragedy. Both remain at the heart of who he is as a wrestling coach at Fight Ready Gym in Scottsdale, Arizona, and as a promoter for MMA fighters and co-owner of World Fight Federation (WFF).

Raised in Tucson, Arizona, Thom comes from a family of fighters. His father, Richard Ortiz, was a boxer in the US Marines after wrestling in high school, and Thom had three older brothers: Eddie, Richard, and Bobby. When Eddie was twelve, he told his father he wanted to box too, but Richard responded by taking him to the wrestling coach at his son's school, Apollo Junior High. "This is better for you," Richard told Eddie regarding wrestling. "You're too young to get hit in the head. I want you to learn how to wrestle.

If you ever want to box in the future, you can look at it later." From there, Eddie went on to be a champion at Sunnyside High School and later an all-American wrestler at Arizona State University.

That inspired Thom to also pursue wrestling. When he was eight, his father put him on the same wrestling team as Bobby, who was then in seventh grade. "I wrestled kids twelve and thirteen years old at Apollo for six years!" Thom said. "When I went to ninth grade at Sunnyside, I wanted to become a champion, too, and then go to college to wrestle."

But that dream was severely challenged when Bobby died of an aneurysm when Thom was just fourteen. It happened while Thom was on his way to a wrestling tournament. "I went to weigh-ins, came back, and found out he had passed into heaven," Thom said with tears welling in his eyes. "I was so angry about losing my brother, but wrestling saved me because after practice every day, I was tired and went home to bed." But the other seven months of the year, when wrestling season was over, Thom got into trouble, turning to alcohol to escape his pain. "Because of Mom and Dad's Mexican heritage, I knew culturally you didn't go outside the family with such problems. You took care of it yourself. 'Drink more beers and figure it out, but work hard' was the expression I lived by," Thom said.

That's when a friend suggested he visit a gym where boxing and jiu-jitsu were being taught, and Thom started training there outside of wrestling season. "I didn't want to go run in the streets anymore. It's simple. It's so simple the government should be involved. As an adult now, I believe this concept of offering kids free after-school programs to wrestle and do other sports is empowering to young people," Thom said. Because he never received counseling when he was young, Thom sometimes struggled to get ahead of his anger and the fear of what he would do in the future because of the pain he experienced, but the grinding team workouts and focused goals to succeed helped him overcome. He compiled an amazing 95–2 record as a wrestler at Sunnyside, earning him Wrestler of the Year honors from *The Arizona Republic,* and he led his team to two consecutive state titles. He graduated from Sunnyside in 1987 with a wrestling scholarship to ASU.

When Thom got to college, his coach made sure he had his priorities in order. "He told us the number one thing was to get your degree. Number two was wrestling, and number three was social life—but you can only do two of those things really well." Thom heeded the advice, becoming a three-time all-American with 118 victories in several weight classes, and was a member of ASU's 1988 national championship team. When he graduated in 1990, Thom served as a coaching assistant for the school, but he then left for ten months to use his degree in finance to become a stockbroker.

> *"He told us the number one thing was to get your degree. Number two was wrestling, and number three was social life—but you can only do two of those things really **well**."*

Thom's heart, though, was still in wrestling, and he stayed in touch with others in the sport. "Bobby Douglas, who was an Olympic competitor and coach, was a longtime mentor of mine and happened to be the Iowa State University coach. In 1992 they needed an interim coach, so Coach Bobby offered me the assistant position, and I moved to Iowa for nine years," Thom said. By then Thom was married, and when his first child, Olivia, was born, Thom asked Coach Bobby what it would take for him to become a head coach. Thom was advised to get a master's degree, and he started classes right away at Iowa State, ultimately receiving his master's degree in industrial relations. By then the stress from his work and school had taken its toll on his personal life. He continued drinking, and his marriage ended in a divorce. Thom remained in Iowa and developed another relationship before accepting his dream job in 2001 returning to Arizona to become the head wrestling coach at ASU. That relationship continued long distance, and within a year Thom's daughter, Sophia, was born and she remained with her mother in Iowa.

About three months after Thom left Iowa, his first daughter, Olivia, who was now five years old, told her mother she wanted to live closer to her father. His ex-wife moved to Arizona with Olivia. "It's a unique thing to be in love with sports, but it takes a special person to recognize that, so my relationships suffered. My time was always taken." Thom stayed focused on his new career and established a reputation as an excellent coach and recruiter. He continued the ASU winning tradition in wrestling, earning coach of the year three times and winning three Pacific 10 conference titles through 2008. The following year, though, the team finished poorly, leading to his dismissal.

When Thom was coaching at ASU, he worked with several excellent wrestlers, such as Cain Velasquez, Brian Bader, and C. B. Dolloway, who continued their careers to become MMA greats while still using their proficient wrestling skills in competition. "Cain's the one who got me started later into watching and training with MMA fighters, so I could compete as a mixed martial artist and apply those same techniques into my coaching," he said. "Combat sports became my new sport that I was passionate about doing, and I love seeing fighters that seem to have no other way out use combat sports to change their lives. If you take away this sport, where would they be?" Thom said, smiling with pride.

Thom continued to immerse himself in these skills while drawing from his previous experience as a kid with his father, punching a bag in the backyard to the wisdom of working with Coach Bobby, who also had a strong martial arts background. "I was getting all of this divine guidance," Thom said, "but it's all about listening to it." After losing his position at ASU, Thom continued to move forward with his goals. He married his second wife, Brandy Pierce, and became a promoter and coach for WFF. He joined his friend, former ASU assistant coach and businessman Al Fuentes, who was co-owner of WFF with Thom. "One door closes, a thousand will open! Now I train fighters for the UFC," Thom said.

The first significant door for Thom opened in 2009, when WFF was scheduled to host its first-ever event at Casino del Sol, located on the Pascua Yaqui Tribe reservation near Tucson. When Thom and Al started WFF, professional MMA fights in the state of

Arizona were just beginning to gain popularity, so the chance to present a show on the reservation was quite an opportunity. "Our background was in educating college kids in wrestling, and we just wanted to bring the same model of organized competition into the MMA world and introduce it in Arizona," Thom said. The first show was on October 3, 2009, and only one hundred tickets had been sold. "The marketing guy at the casino wanted to cancel it because of security costs, but Al and I reached out to the military. We promoted by radio. Al got on the internet, and we made it happen. About one thousand veterans came from Tucson that night!"

Together, with their wives who joined them in business, Thom and Al had to overcome many trials to launch the WFF. Thom's new wife, Brandy, was ready to give birth to their first child when Thom's father, Richard, had passed away. That same weekend, Thom was cornering Cain in a fight; then two days later their son was born—this all happened just two weeks before the big event at Casino Del Sol. However, Thom and Al conquered these difficulties. Propelled by the success of the Tucson event, they grew from there and have promoted more than thirty-seven events through the end of 2017. As a fight promoter for WFF, another door swung open for Thom to create huge opportunities for fighters like Ramon Salazar, Joe Mendez, Patrick Williams, Frankie Saenz, and Benny Madrid, all of whom benefitted from Thom's personal coaching guidance and the professional organizational support of WFF. "Benny has an amazing story and goes to talk with kids in South Phoenix who have families in and out of prison," Thom said. "He was a drug dealer at one time and had served prison time because of selling OxyContin pills. Benny tells these kids, 'If I didn't get off the pills, I wouldn't be able to fight.' He's become a productive member of society, and MMA is what changed his life."

Thom is grateful as well for the new path he developed for himself through MMA, because the stability it brought opened a third door for him to overcome a serious alcohol addiction. Early in his wrestling coaching career, Thom was drinking and driving when there was a collision. He wasn't wearing a seatbelt, but another student with him in the vehicle was almost killed by the strap of the seatbelt he was wearing. Thom only received a deep cut on his forehead from the implosion of the windshield. "The authorities said I was lucky," he said, shaking his head. "I'm an addict, but I got help from God and my counselor, Mindy Bail, and I've had no drinking in my life now for almost seven years." Thom's faith remains vital to his sobriety. "Ultimately, it has to be God. He gets the glory for changing my life. If anything good comes to me, it's God. If anything comes to me in a negative light, I generated it with my thoughts. Jesus already died for me on the cross, so any pain and struggle is created in my own mind."

"Our background was in educating college kids in wrestling, and we just wanted to bring the same model of organized competition into the MMA world and introduce it in Arizona."

*   *   *

Developing a strong team to help other fighters overcome their personal weaknesses to succeed as athletes and in life has been strategic for WFF and the Fight Ready Gym. Al helps Thom with business organization and is a performance coach, assisting fighters in strengthening physical issues. Brandy, now Thom's ex-wife, is sole owner and chief financial officer of WFF. As of 2018, she is also the state's only female MMA promoter and a former naturopathic doctor who works with fighters to assist them with their standard medical tests while organizing behind-the-scenes details for all their events. Thom calls on veteran cut man Robbie Munroe to work WFF fights as well as other coaches from the Fight Ready Gym. "All of these super people come together to make it happen."

Thom says it's important for fighters to learn the formal processes required by each state for their career. He guides them through mandatory medical information vital to their safety, helps them find places to go for medical testing and physicals, and shows them how to do all of this in a way that's simple and effective for them. "MMA continues to succeed as a sport, and as WFF grows, I will continue to be a great matchmaker to place the right fighters in the right matches—I pray, and they show up," Thom said. His future desire is to use his degree in human resource management to set up a customized system of procedures individualized for each fighter to help them set up personal insurance, retirement planning, and prepare for their future as a professional fighter. But Thom and his team at WFF aren't quite there yet internally to offer all these services. "These guys need a process to follow. They have families. Fighting is hard work, and when they win, they need help to have stewardship over their money to practice delayed gratification and use their income wisely," Thom said. "When you get hit here," pointing at the center of his forehead, "it's the executive process thinking part of your brain that is directly affected, and that's where guys get hit first. That's why I will never let my kids box. People make fun of Mayweather because of his elusive fighting style, but he never gets hit. That's smart!"

As he's worked with MMA fighters over the years, Thom says most are well-trained athletes who are generally more laid back, not the general public perception that they're bullies or "… loud mouths getting off the barstools. Conor McGregor may bring more people in to view the fights because of his wild tactics, but that's just the way it is," he said. "I know a lot of MMA purists who are trainers and don't like the hype, but if anyone wants to put eyeballs in front of the cage, we have to do it. More eyes equal more sponsors with direct monies. I'm convinced my sincere relationship with the fighters can help them decide what is best done with their resources."

Thom hopes the positive publicity WFF is gaining will bring in more income so he can help direct it to causes that benefit children in crisis situations. "There's a misconception about the money in this business being so big, but we're smart with what we earn, and our organization is profitable," Thom said. "I'm just thankful for the fighters we have and the opportunity to work with them. I have a two-bedroom apartment and live simply. Francesca Battistelli sings in 'He Knows My Name,' 'I don't need my name in lights. I'm famous in my Father's eyes,' and that's good enough for me." Thom is also put off by naysayers who believe he is dishonest because he's a promoter. "I've been called a snake, but I *do* care about these guys, and I honor them. People are not to be used. America has a love for things and money instead of people. That's the real problem."

> *"I know a lot of MMA purists who are trainers and don't like the hype, but if anyone wants to put eyeballs in front of the cage, we have to do it. More eyes equal more sponsors with direct monies."*

*   *   *

Thom has been honored with selection into both the ASU Sports Hall of Fame and Pima County Sports Hall of Fame. He continues to prioritize three major life roles that serve to inspire family, friends, and others in his community, all while giving credit to God for his ongoing relationships with individuals. First, he is the father of two young boys with Brandy, and he keeps them active in sports because of the positive influence he believes it has on their lives.

"My five-year-old knew how to float and swim at age three, and my seven-year-old has been involved in chess club, gymnastics, and swim club since he was five. Whatever sport he chooses to do, he will succeed because he's a natural athlete," Thom said. "My daughter, Olivia, is twenty-two and has played volleyball eleven months out of the year since she was twelve. People would tell me, 'She's gonna burn herself out,' but I always said, 'No, she's not, because she has energy.'" She went to Benedictine University of Mesa to play center and coordinate other volleyball teams while getting her education.

She is scheduled to graduate in May 2018. Sophia is attending high school in Iowa, and they keep in touch.

Second, as a coach, Thom believes kids should join wrestling at about age twelve, but if he or she is eight or younger, he suggests gymnastics or swimming to learn body control. "I worked with a couple of foster kids. Both parents were abusive, so we tried to break the cycle and taught the kids jiu-jitsu, but it was too much for the six-year-old. He was very angry, so swimming was a good alternative," Thom said. He's looking to start an organization to get kids who are in challenging life situations involved in sports. He's doing this because he feels several factors, such as addiction and divorce, are difficult on children, and athletic activity helps them cope. "Even my own son, at age five, had troubles when his mother and I divorced. I took him to see a counselor, and she told me, 'Your son is whining and acting like a two-year-old, but kids will go back to where the change or trauma took place and act out from that. It's what they knew at the time when things drastically changed.' She says my son is now handling the divorce okay, but to also keep in touch with what's going on. It reminds me of my own displaced anger from losing my brother and other life situations I've worked through."

Finally, as an athlete, Thom understands everyone wants to be involved with something, whether it is a gang, baseball, wrestling, or some other sport. "It's a group of kids, a team—it's association. If you separate kids from their athletics, you'll have more gang activity," he said. "My gang was the wrestling team; it was my group. The US is fortunate to be a country that has sports and education together in the same school. If we have the opportunity to financially back it and support kids in these ways, who cares how it's done."

He also continues to encourage youths and fans of all ages as a competitive fighter. In February 2018, at age fifty-one, Thom fought well but lost to Andy Perez, who won the WFF lightweight championship. It was a close fight, with clinches, punches, and knockdowns from both fighters. "We can only be as good as we push ourselves to be—nothing less, past the limits, never stop, do one more, be happy, make money, and give back," Thom said. He will be moving down to the featherweight division and plans to keep fighting.

> *"It's a group of kids, a team—it's association.*
> *If you separate kids from their athletics,*
> *you'll have more gang activity. My gang*
> *was the wrestling team; it was my group."*

As a fighter who has returned to the octagon, Thom wants to continue utilizing the skills of MMA professional fighters to inspire and influence children through personal time and training as they participate with or watch the fighters, trainers, or staff at Fight Ready Gym. He had one foster child at the gym who met Patrick Williams, a UFC bantamweight, before returning to his family. Patrick got to know the child for a month while he trained, and now Patrick misses him. "The boy watched him win his fight in twenty-one seconds and saw Patrick exalted inside the octagon," Thom said. "When the boy returned to his family, he was different. This child got to be around and sit next to this UFC fighter who was humble and even thankful for the food he ate.

It made an impact on him. He received a signed poster, hat, and shirt that everyone on the team signed for him."

Thom volunteers his time at the Boys and Girls Club, Pascua Yaqui Tribe, and heads up wrestling seminars for kids. He does this to serve the community, and it does much to promote more knowledge about the MMA industry. "I want to be in a position to help hundreds, hopefully thousands, of people, but I know my time is limited," Thom admitted. "Making money is important, but I can spend it on these kids. People are busy with life, but if I can recruit good foster parents to create a program and make it simple with what to do and design the legal forms to do it, kids can enjoy the experience of what team looks like, and MMA can change and influence lives."

In the end, Thom believes the MMA industry can be a positive force worldwide to decrease crime, and reduce conflict in many communities. He is always looking for unique out-of-the-cage ways to help others. "God gave us free will, so knowing my soul is forever, if I go tomorrow, I'm okay with that because I have endured much. But if I make it to be one hundred years old, great! I just want to take care of my family, and I'm glad I get to enjoy this journey during the rest of my lifetime."

Wilson Reis

PERSISTENT TO LEARN AND
ALWAYS ON THE MOVE

Brazilian Wilson Reis has always been in motion. As an MMA fighter, he's gone from one organization to another in three different weight classifications to earn an outstanding 22–8–0 record, competing most recently as a flyweight in UFC. As a young boy, he never stopped moving after kicking aside his soccer ball to emulate the martial arts he saw in Bruce Lee movies. And as a small child, first in tiny Bonito de Minas and later in big city Sao Paulo, Wilson kept busy going to school and helping take care of his two brothers while his parents labored to scrape together what they could for the family.

It shouldn't be surprising, then, that Wilson was even on the move the day he and his twin brother were born.

"There was no hospital in Bonito de Minas, a very small city of ten thousand, so they traveled to the nearest one, which was about three hours away on a very bad road," Wilson said. At the end of the bumpy journey, Wilson and his brother, Dilson, were born. Once the family returned to Bonito de Minas, his mother took care of the twins while his father worked in Sao Paulo, sending money home and visiting when he could. The commute eventually became too difficult, so they moved to Sao Paulo when the boys were two years old. His brother Wagner was born a year later.

"They both had to work," Wilson said of his parents, "so Dilson and I had to be by ourselves at the house when we were about five and my little brother was three. It was very hard for them to make that decision, but when we started school, it got better." The boys went to school on their own, but Wilson said his father prepared them well. "Dad taught us how to take care of ourselves, handle the streets, and how to talk to strangers when needed. We had to walk through the city to get to the bus location. We learned how to take care of each other," he said.

The boys always held hands when crossing the hectic streets of the city. But there was one time when seven-year-old Wagner suddenly let go of his brother's hand and darted forward into a crowded intersection. Wilson couldn't get to him in time. "It was only seconds when he got hit by a car," Wilson exclaimed. "It was like slow motion. I saw the guy hit my brother, but it was like an angel was holding him somehow because the car hit his backpack. He went rolling about six times in the street, and then he just got up and started walking!" Wilson and Dilson ran over to Wagner. "Everybody was yelling. I looked at his head for blood, a cut or something, but there was nothing. We were hugging him, and it was very emotional."

"He got hit hard by the car. It was God who made him bounce off the wheels because he could have died right there," Wilson said. "Finally, we got to the bus stop on the other side, and everyone looking at Wagner knew it was a miracle that he was even alive. My parents were amazed too. I can only imagine how they felt. We shared the feeling of maybe losing Wagner, whom we all loved. I remember how insane it was! It's still hard to think about."

When away from the dangerous city streets, Wilson, like most boys in Brazil, spent his days playing soccer, but when his Uncle Edson introduced him to martial arts movies featuring Bruce Lee, he was hooked. Wilson loved watching how the actors participated in actual tournament matches, so he started learning and practicing some of the moves. When he was twelve, his mother worked as a maid for a well-to-do Japanese Brazilian family who had practiced judo and karate for generations. One day, while cleaning the house, she saw a gi, a traditional white martial arts uniform with a belt, and the wife gave it to her as a gift. "There were three of us kids, but only one gi," Wilson said, "and she knew I was crazy about the sport, so she gave it to me!"

Uniform in hand, Wilson went to work to find a place where he could begin to learn martial arts formally. "Everybody who watched the movies wanted to become a fighter, but I needed to find a gym because my brothers and I weren't allowed to fight in the house. So I found a place where I could take a class every Saturday," Wilson said. Before long, though, Wilson discovered that his instructor was not an actual martial arts coach and discerned that such casual training wasn't going to take his skills to higher levels. Since every city in Brazil has a training center to ensure children have an opportunity to get started in sports, Wilson started there. He was one of more than five thousand kids on a waiting list, but after a couple of months he was registered into a class. The only martial arts choices were karate or judo. He opted for judo because the moves were similar to what he saw in the movies, and there was both training and the opportunity to fight other students. Wilson said sparring was both fascinating and nerve-wracking, but he was thrilled when he won matches. "After my first big tournament, I came home with a bronze medal. It was great, and my parents supported me."

After that, anything that said "martial arts" got Wilson's attention. "If I saw a newspaper or magazine, I would buy it," he said. "I bought a VCR tape about the Gracie jiu-jitsu academy in California and saw they wore a similar gi as I did for judo." Gracie jiu-jitsu began nearly a century ago in Brazil, when Helio Gracie, a physically frail young boy, learned from his older brother traditional jiu-jitsu techniques brought to the country from Japan by Esai Maeda. Helio modified what he was taught to develop skills that enabled him to defend himself against much larger opponents, and those skills quickly became the new expression of jiu-jitsu in Brazil. Wilson felt judo gave him a solid base of knowledge about grappling moves and takedowns, but after watching the tape a couple of times, he knew he had to find a different gym to learn jiu-jitsu. Incredibly, he found a Gracie jiu-jitsu center close to home (currently one of only two remaining in South America) but knew his parents didn't have the money to afford his membership, so Wilson got creative.

"I told myself, 'If I tell my parents they have to pay, they're gonna *take* me out. But if I don't pay the gym, they're gonna *kick* me out.' So I did the wrong thing and kept lying to the gym, saying, 'I'm gonna pay next week,' like a delayed rent. As far as I could extend it, I did it." The Gracie instructor knew Wilson was a thirteen-year-old kid with no money and saw how much he liked to train, so he allowed him to stay in return for working at the facility. At Gracie, Wilson found that unlike in judo tournaments, where he fought well but didn't win often because he had to compete against others with higher expertise, the jiu-jitsu students fought each other at tournaments according to belt level and weight.

"That was the real beginning of success for me," he said, adding that it was fun to be "a crazy, nosey kid" interacting with older guys on the squad. After training, they often enjoyed a bowl of acai, a popular fruit treat in Brazil, and the acai store was located next to an outlet of Bad Boy clothing. "Bad Boy was a big company, especially in martial arts. I was fascinated with everything inside," Wilson said, smiling. "The acai store owner liked me and listened to me, and he also knew the Bad Boy store licensee, so he asked for clothing to give to me and for patches to put on my gi. That's when everything started, at age fourteen. I saw my future and knew I would be a professional fighter."

Soon, in addition to training at Gracie, Wilson knew he wanted to expand his training to allow him to fight internationally, so he started going to a second gym, where he gained skills and earned new belt levels in competition while working there in exchange for not paying fees. The gym was formed by a partnership between then-friends and professional fighters Jorge Patino, also known as "Macaco," and Roberto Godoi. Their credibility allowed their students to compete all over Brazil and participate in international tournaments. Wilson trained with Godoi, and by age sixteen he traveled abroad for the first time with the gym's team to compete in the Pan American Jiu-jitsu Championships in the United States. However, when Godoi and Macaco had a falling out later that same year, Wilson had a decision to make. "By then I had been training three years with coach Godoi, yet the guy I looked up to was Macaco. But I wanted a career, and I knew I really needed coach Godoi. He showed me how much he cared," Wilson said. "It was a smart move. I prayed to become a great fighter, and Godoi has never changed his belief in me. From then until now, seventeen years, he is still my coach and corners me in every fight I have and all through my camps."

> *"The acai store owner liked me and listened to me, and he also knew the Bad Boy store licensee, so he asked for clothing to give to me and for patches to put on my gi. That's when everything started, at age fourteen. I saw my future and knew I would be a professional fighter."*

*   *   *

When Wilson was in the US training in Philadelphia, he was introduced to another combatant, Jared Weiner, who owned a gym near Philadelphia called BJJ United (the BJJ stands for Brazilian jiu-jitsu). Jared also spoke Portuguese, and he and Wilson became friends. When Jared later traveled to Brazil in 2004 to train and compete at the same event with Wilson at the month-long World Jiu-Jitsu Championship tournament in Rio de Janeiro, they shared housing. "If you ever want to come to Philadelphia," Jared told him, "I'd love to have you there." When Wilson won the world championship as a brown belt at age nineteen, it took him only a moment to make a major decision that would have him on the move once again.

"I went back home and told my dad, 'I want to move to the United States.' He said 'Hey, I really want you to go—I don't have money to buy a ticket or anything, but I will support you.' Then my true friends from the gym said they would give me the money and I could work it off and pay them later. So in one month's time I told my parents, got the money to go, and that was it. I was headed to the US to chase my dream!" Wilson said, grinning ear to ear. He then asked a friend who knew English to send an email to Jared to let him know he would be in Philadelphia the next week. "It was only a short time after the tournament, so Jared was really surprised, but I told him I would be at the airport," Wilson said. "At that time it was November, and coach Godoi knew he was going to present me with my black belt in December. He told me, 'I'm giving you your black belt now because you've earned it. Go see what you can do, and live the fighter's dream!' I was so happy I was a black belt! I received it that morning and flew out that night."

Wilson only had a six-month tourist visa, so he had to return to Brazil and then go back and forth several times for the next few years because he could only participate as an amateur athlete without pay. Wilson won many Brazilian jiu-jitsu titles in both gi and no-gi divisions during that time, but he knew he wanted to become a paid professional athlete and was determined to live permanently in the US. He asked Jared to help him learn English and also worked side jobs in construction when he was in the States to have the money to compete in high-level tournaments. Wilson continued to fight well and quickly established a name for himself in the American media. This credibility in jiu-jitsu was essential in helping him receive a work visa to live permanently in the US. Certain applicants can file as "persons with extraordinary ability" in the sciences, arts, education, business, or athletics, but they must have extensive documentation showing sustained national or international acclaim and recognition in their fields of expertise. They must also acquire someone in the States to sponsor them.

"So in one month's time I told my parents, got the money to go, and that was it. I was headed to the US to chase my dream!"

"I found a lawyer and gave her a jiu-jitsu magazine to show her the article that proved I was a really good," Wilson said. "Jared became my sponsor because he had the gym, and I was going to be an instructor there." Through the lawyer, Wilson got his work visa and moved to the US to stay in 2007. "I saw that I had a future," he said, his eyes sparkling, "and I believed I could now make a living being a professional fighter."

Wilson then took his jiu-jitsu to a new level, combining new skills in striking learned at BJJ United and beginning to fight in MMA bouts. He stacked up a three-fight winning streak and then debuted for the EliteXC organization on their *ShoXC* series in January 2008. He continued with three more wins and was crowned as the first and only EliteXC bantamweight champion on September 26, 2008. He moved to Bellator with another win in June 2009, at which time he was introduced to Dominick Cruz, who was then in WEC and working with another WEC fighter in Philadelphia. "Dominick and I were talking and he said, 'You should come out to Alliance MMA in San Diego.' Then he called me to help work in his training camp, which meant I was on Dominick's team to help him train for a fight with Joseph Benevidez because Benevidez was a southpaw like me. He paid for my flight and everything, and it was also the first time I talked to Eric Del Fierro, head coach at Alliance. I trained with Dominick, and he won the bout, which set up his championship fight with Brian Bowles," Wilson said. Again on the move, Wilson went to California to train for every camp after that.

Dominick's training regimen and development of a personal fighting style of being elusive and hard to hit intrigued Wilson. It was strange to him, with fancy footwork, feints (or fake moves), punches, and kicks combined with extremely active head movement to dodge strikes. Wilson always believed he pushed himself in training, but Dominick was at whole other level. "If my coach is pushing me and saying, 'Hit your head on the wall; it's going to be good,' I'll do it, but not without being told first," Wilson said. "Yet Dominick is getting pushed by his coach, and I think he pushes himself three times more! That's what makes the difference in him. I'm always amazed."

Wilson is convinced Dominick's training tenacity and superior skills led to him becoming a champion in the WEC, and after his two title defenses, the organization merged with the UFC, where he earned two more title defenses before dealing with a career-threatening injury. "Everything that happened to him, with his injuries and double ACL surgery, then losing the belt, seemed like nothing during his first comeback win by knockout. He got injured again with another ACL surgery but made another great return in 2016 to win the championship belt back. Next, he defended the belt again but then later lost it, all in the same year," Wilson said. "Dominick is very good motivation for me because there are times when too much is put in front of us, but at the end of the day it's on me. I say yes or no. I can always do more, but I want to do it better and never quit."

*   *   *

Looking back to his early childhood and forward over his career, Wilson believes he's always been on the move, chasing his dreams, and he feels that's what combat sports are all about. When kids ask him about MMA as a career, he tells them it's a long road. "Kids should find the right gym with a good coach to guide them, and professional fighters too," he said. "But they should focus, as a student of training, first in one martial art at a time, like jiu-jitsu, until they are confident in their skills." They can then transition into the other forms of MMA, he believes, so they can learn the moves for each sport because it's hard to remember everything. "To make a career last, they will want to find their good disciplines. It took me a while to find jiu-jitsu and then so long until I got my black belt. It takes hard work to become a champion," Wilson said. "When I was young in jiu-jitsu, every day after training while walking home I said to myself, 'Today was a good day. I had a good class.' And the next day, if I had a bad day like getting tapped out ten times, I still kept going."

He uses the same mind-set today in training camp before each fight, moving forward through the struggles of maintaining diet, managing fatigue, and striving for mental focus. "I sometimes think, 'Maybe I should move on to something else to save my body from boot camps.' But I've been doing this my whole life, and that doubt is temporary—it lasts only for a few minutes. So I go to the next training each day, go to sleep that night, and make the weight cut the next morning, all while strictly managing how much I eat and drink. Then, the final day before the fight, I get to fully rehydrate and eat several small meals after weigh-in, and I forget about everything except the fight," Wilson said, laughing at the intense nature of the buildup. "The next day comes, I fight my best fight, and just want to do it all again. I get all caught up in the process and then ask my coach, 'When can I do this again?' I was born to do this and have found my talent."

Some kids from his jiu-jitsu team in Brazil were talented, too, but were not allowed to continue in the sport as they got older because they were told by their parents that they had to attend college or go to work for a company. "My friends couldn't live their dreams," Wilson said, "and now they see me today and say, 'Man, I could have been like that.' I knew as a fourteen-year-old I needed the best school of martial arts, and I went after it while my parents supported me. That taught me to be very humble. I worked hard for everything." He and his brothers remained close as they grew up and have remained so in the decade since he left to live in the US. "I tried to bring both my brothers here because I wanted them to be able to experience the different life and language, but I feel like Wagner and Dilson didn't want the American life," said Wilson. "Dilson is a black belt, too, and was able to get a visa to come to the US to fight, but he decided to go back home after three years. Wagner doesn't like to fight and was the troubled one—drinking, partying, and losing good opportunities. Two times his visa got denied because the process is very strict. But he's doing good now with his baby and a family in Brazil."

Wilson faced obstacles like lack of funding, challenges securing his travel visas, and being away from his family at a young age. But he never allowed them to be excuses and then trained and worked diligently to compete in several organizations before making it into the UFC. "People need to understand how hard it is to become a professional fighter and to make a living," he said. "But I tell people that anything can happen in life and encourage them to keep moving forward, study the sport, and not to focus on the money, because it looks like more than there is. It's a beautiful sport that will teach you how to overcome."

> *"The next day comes, I fight my best fight, and just want to do it all again. I get all caught up in the process and then ask my coach, 'When can I do this again?' I was born to do this and have found my talent."*

Though Wilson has overcome much, he said his biggest challenge by far was his divorce. He and his ex-wife met in high school and were together for six years before being married for seven more years. "It's something really personal," Wilson said, staring down at his hands. "She said there was no more future in us. She found somebody else and wanted a divorce. I thought it was going to be okay after our separation for about six months because I gave her a chance to come back, but she didn't want to. Then later, when she wanted to attempt getting back together, she gave me a chance to reconsider, but I was hurt and didn't want it, so she decided that was it," said Wilson. "After one month I looked to reach out to her again, but it was over." It was especially hard, Wilson said, the first year after the divorce, and there were days he'd get upset when he saw something that reminded him of her. But it got better, and it doesn't hurt anymore if he sees her.

"Little by little, I have begun to see the things I did wrong and messed up. But the craziest thing is, when our relationship started to get really bad, it was the best time in my career," he said, shaking his head. "I wondered why. I fought in all these events in the beginning of my career with no paycheck, but she was there. I figure maybe the attention wasn't there for her. Perhaps she was scared of where I was going as a professional fighter in the UFC." He said they argued a lot during training camp because she wanted to go out, but he'd be tired and not want to. "I'd look back and think, 'But I'm working so hard to make money for our family.' Yet she's a woman, and she has her needs, and I was so focused on my career I didn't see it. I couldn't make it work, and I can't go back now, but I give her points because she really stuck with me in all the camps and everything. At first I just blamed her, but now I look back and see it was fifty-fifty."

Personal relationships are hard for fighters, Wilson believes, because there are so many things that can derail their careers. He recalls how he lost a big fight when he and his wife were first separated, and he felt he couldn't share what was going on with anybody. When he finally told Coach Eric on the way to weigh-ins, "… he was real upset and said, 'Why didn't you tell me? We could have pulled out of the fight!' I told him I thought I was ready to fight, but he knew I wasn't," Wilson said. "After I lost the bout, he said, 'I don't know what's happening, but I have to know.' A coach needs to know the personal stuff so they know where your mind is; otherwise, something like that could happen again."

After losing that fight in 2015, Wilson went home to Bonito de Minas for the first time in twenty years. He gave his parents some money to repair and move back into their old house in the center of the city. Bonito de Minas had grown, he said, and when he and his mother walked through his childhood neighborhood, kids were pointing at him because he was famous. Yet he noticed the city had increased facilities for sports like soccer but nothing new for martial arts. "I saw a gym and met the owner who said I could work out, but there was no MMA equipment. I asked him, 'Why don't you put mats in here to give the kids something to do?' He bought mats and bags but needed more assistance, so I supplied gis and gloves from Bad Boy," Wilson said. "We have a team in Bonito de Minas that I connected with Godoi's gym, G13BJJ (meaning Godoi 2013 Brazilian Jiu-jitsu), in Sao Paulo so they are affiliated and can now compete outside the state."

> "I remember my first year as a black belt, thinking about what's next, and I have even more fire than before! There's always something I am going after, event to event, and I constantly desire more—it drives me every day."

Wilson inspires the kids there by sending them videos and telling them to invite others so they can earn G13BJJ gis from Sao Paulo through good school grades or work at home. "What I really want there is a big gym that not only has classes but will feed the students and offer more services for their families. The town is very humble, with a lot of people who need help, and the mayor is assisting me," Wilson said. "Encouraging students to compete in jiu-jitsu can lead to a job as an instructor and maybe into a professional fighting career. I want to stay engaged with them because it's important to me, and I will be more actively involved later as an instructor, especially after I retire."

In his early thirties, Wilson hopes he has ten more bouts in him before his professional fighting career ends. "When I retire it will be because I *have* to retire. I never want to be in the situation as one of those guys that *should* retire, but they're still fighting for a paycheck," Wilson said. "I'm doing great in my career, so I can be smart with my investments in other things. My focus is to be the best I can be to earn and save as much money as possible."

From being a young boy practicing Bruce Lee movements in his living room to being a professional martial artist in the octagon, Wilson has always been on the move. Wilson admits, though, that it scares him to even think about quitting someday. But he also realizes that eventually, everything stops. "I remember my first year as a black belt, thinking about what's next, and I have even more fire than before! There's always something I am going after, event to event, and I constantly desire more—it drives me every day. But you're never going to know everything. There's always a new technique to chase or a tournament to win," Wilson said. "It's the learning of new things—that's what moves me to become better. Although my fighting career will end, I will do martial arts for the rest of my life."

Jansen Azarias

*DISCIPLINED FROM YOUTH TO
CULTIVATE OTHERS*

Jansen Azarias was born to be a fierce yet humble warrior who sets others free from peril. He developed the combatant aspects early in life, in the town of Marikina, located along the eastern border of Metro Manila in the Philippines. His father grew up in the streets of the Philippines, living and breathing the multiple disciplines of martial arts to survive, so he taught everything he knew to his son, starting when Jansen was very young.

"He showed me his fighting skills from street experience, which is the best kind. My dad also loved boxing, so I watched fights with him, and during commercials he would train me. It's one of the few fond memories of him, and most afternoons he and I would spar with sticks, where the only lesson I learned was that it hurts." Jansen said. "I was a little kid with asthma and severe ADHD; then at five years old the doctors told my parents I was a 'special' child with borderline autism spectrum disorder, also called Asperger's syndrome. I displayed disruptive behaviors, opposition, aggressive movements, and consistent panic with anxiety. My social isolation led to difficulty reading or talking until I was about six years old, so to all my siblings and cousins my nickname was *engot*, the Filipino equivalent of 'idiot.' Because of my issues, martial arts was something that my parents and the teachers in school thought would be really good for me."

In physical education (PE) class, he was exposed to formal escrima, or arnis, a traditional martial art of the Philippines, which uses weapon-based fighting with sticks, knives, blades, and other weapons as well as open-hand techniques without weapons. By the time he was in high school, Jansen had also mastered tae kwon do. He engaged in multiple martial arts, such as dumog, a Filipino form of wrestling while standing upright; aikido, a Japanese system of throwing, joint-locking, striking, and pinning techniques, with weapons included; muay thai, a Thailand form of stand-up striking with combined use of fists, elbows, knees, and shins; and judo and Japanese jiu-jitsu. One day someone told him about the Gracie family, who established Brazilian jiu-jitsu. "I was very familiar with Japanese jiu-jitsu, but when I saw Royce Gracie win his fight, there was an eight-man elimination with no breaks in between. I was amazed it was an all-in-one-day tournament!"

When Jansen watched that Gracie tournament when he was twelve years old, it was his first experience seeing mixed martial arts. He graduated high school early at age fifteen and was fully immersed in and competitive in multiple martial arts by the time he entered college at the University of Manila. "In my beginning studies, I loved the philosophy behind the books of the samurai, and then, of course, I became a fan of Bruce Lee," he said. Later, as he watched the new style of MMA matches with sport pioneers Tito Ortiz and Ken Shamrock, he was entertained by the competitive atmosphere and how they found the most effective parts of martial arts to use in a bout. But Jansen had mixed feelings because he felt like the philosophical and mental aspects of martial arts were missing from MMA.

During college Jansen got together with his best friends, Ray and Alex, and they all trained in multiple forms of martial arts. "We really wouldn't do some of those in any other setting than a dojo, but we had fun," he said. They added in Freerunning, an acrobatic and athletic discipline of jumping, grabbing, and climbing walls, daily in the park during lunch and then again after school. "Since computer science was our class of study at the university, where few other students had the same passion about martial arts, we naturally got to know each other better. But we were also the top hackers in our class and definitely juvenile delinquents," Jansen said, laughing.

*   *   *

Jansen came to the United States in 2006, when he was eighteen, moving to Tucson, Arizona, because his father's former boss had moved there too. "My dad worked in the US as an accountant, and he traveled to and from the states frequently. He had become a citizen many years before meeting my mom, then returned early to the Philippines to retire," Jansen said. "As a gift for my sixteenth birthday, Dad established the paperwork acknowledging me as his son, making me a legal US citizen." Jansen said he moved from the Philippines to America to "pursue something," along with the reality of fleeing from his parents and the college he hated. "I was failing college and didn't want my parents to know; I was trying to escape the consequences from all the lies about skipping classes. That was my plan. Pursuing my vague dreams as I ran away from my hard reality, that was the truth," he said, looking off to the side.

Tucson became Jansen's new home as he secured a job at a call center and then immediately found a place he could train in kajukenbo, a form of MMA and street-oriented fighting training that incorporates a blend of striking, kicking, throwing, takedowns, joint locks, and weapon disarmament. "Honestly, I got to the point in my life where most of what I did was not good even though it *looked* that way," he admitted. "The martial arts I practiced were from the place of an addict. I started drinking at age ten and was an alcoholic from age sixteen until twenty. I literally fought my way through a very rough background growing up with my family because my dad was verbally and physically abusive to me and my mom. He was a womanizer who had several families—I couldn't stand that about him and battled the demons with so much anger."

"At eighteen, I was working out four hours a day, including martial arts, because if I didn't do that, I would go insane—it was my chemical of choice, plus about half a bottle of vodka just to sleep at night," Jansen said, shaking his head. "Writing became another addiction, and even though some of these things, like martial arts and writing a journal, looked positive, the drive was very angry. But the fear of taking a chemical substance other than alcohol was unacceptable, and I refused to do that to myself."

Jansen met his wife, Barbie Maestas, just two months after arriving in the US. They came to know each other as they worked together at the call center. Barbie was a single mother, and Jansen started tutoring her ten-year-old son Timmy in math and reading. "I knew I could do that, but then noticed Timmy revealed a lot of anger issues, so I started teaching him martial arts to learn how to cope with his anger. That's how my relationship journey with them started," he said. "Timmy began inviting his friends and cousins, and we would have morning trainings in my apartment. Homework was the most important item to address, though, because almost all of them were failing or behind in school, especially in reading and arithmetic. They all had similar stories—divorced parents, family members in prison or in gangs, drug or alcohol abuse, poverty— and they felt defeated in life and considered their potential to be nothing."

Over the next several months, Jansen and Barbie grew closer, spending time together helping the kids in addition to working full-time, and they started dating. Barbie also introduced him to her friends at church, where their relationship deepened. "I found my wife's crazy to be the kind I like," Jansen said, laughing. "I enjoyed that she was able to break my routine. Normally, I hated breaking up things, but with her it was okay. I thought, 'I can deal with this.' She helped me grow. She showed me what was socially appropriate, how to understand cues in language with sayings, and helped me to read people's intentions. The joke Barbie says about me is, 'You're so smart you can go to the moon, but you can't cross the street.' She tells me that often, but we work so well together. In a sense, she has taught me how to cross the street."

"They all had similar stories—divorced parents, family members in prison or in gangs, drug or alcohol abuse, poverty— and they felt defeated in life and considered their potential to be nothing."

Jansen and Barbie were married in April 2007, and later that year created an organization, emerging out of their shared caring for children, called Higher Ground. "That's when my life really began to change," Jansen said with a smile. He quit running from his past and began to take seriously the faith he was introduced to at church. "At age twenty, I gave my heart to Jesus Christ, and after I gave up drinking completely, things began to get so much better, even reconciling with my dad," he said. "My faith drives a lot of what I do. I always say, 'If it has nothing to do with my calling in my life's purpose, getting closer to God, or nothing to do with my family—I don't want to do it.'" His beliefs drive him constantly forward to become a better person, and he shares his faith with kids and people along his path.

"There is a way to get out of trouble without running away. There is a way to grow and never be hopeless—we just all grow differently." Jansen believes each seed, with a different kind of soil or condition, can become the biggest tree ever. "In a sense, as people, we are all broken, yet we don't need to be fixed, but we need to grow instead. This is my drive and love for what I do, because I'm not 'fixing' anybody but showing them how to grow. All seeds need to break in order to grow. Given the right soil for growth, circumstance, timing, and the right resources to change, I want other people and children to have that—to know they are not stuck. Brokenness doesn't require fixing but requires direction."

As they established Higher Ground Youth Center at Mission View Assembly of God Church, Jansen and Barbie worked together to provide free tutoring in a variety of subjects, recreational activities, and relational support for sixty students, and the children's lives began to blossom. Within two years, there was still a waiting list of fifty kids each year to use their services, so they made Higher Ground a nonprofit organization and began to meet with other community leaders to address further expansion. After their son, Kenji, was born, they made a major decision to quit their jobs and devote themselves full-time to Higher Ground. When their first students graduated from high school, several returned to Higher Ground to join other college students as Life Changers, volunteers dedicated to the Higher Ground mission of "… empowering one life at a time, to reach, transform, and elevate the community through love and building character."

> "There is a way to get out of trouble
> without running away. There is a way to
> grow and never be hopeless—we just
> all grow differently."

Tucson's largest school district, Tucson Unified School District (TUSD), stepped up to partner with Higher Ground in 2011 and provided six classrooms from one of the newly built wings at Valencia Middle School. Higher Ground maxed out the space immediately as it grew to 130 students, with over 40 students on a waiting list. In addition to homework tutoring and math and reading programs, Higher Ground expanded its program to provide tackle football for middle school students; a boxing team; dance, art, and choir teams; high school career internships; character development courses for boys and girls; and financial literacy training.

"We started our boxing program with a new coach and then, outside of that, I had middle school students saying, 'Oh, let's challenge Mr. Jansen,' because I was as small as they were. They all knew I did martial arts, and I was the most agile, climbing walls and freerunning with front and back flips. The kids loved it and saw me as a challenge. For a short time, we said, 'If you get an A, you get to wrestle Mr. Jansen!'" he said. "We had fun, but then the kids began to ask, 'Why don't you teach us martial arts?' Knowing I couldn't teach them kajukenbo or escrima with knife fighting, I began to teach them the wrestling parts of it, and that's how that phase started."

They started practicing grappling on hard tile floors because they couldn't afford mats and did takedowns on the softer grass outside. By then Jansen had also learned some Brazilian jiu-jitsu techniques, but he was grateful they had to wear long sleeves on their gi, the uniform for jiu-jitsu students. "I still hate hugs and feel differently in my skin. Most people don't understand that aspect of my physical condition," Jansen said, rubbing his arms. "So even though I'm hyperaware of what's being done to me because of sensitivity to touch and can literally feel the movements my opponent is trying to secure, I work through those issues and enjoy the sport, even though the close contact required in jiu-jitsu remains strange to me."

* * *

When one of the students found a jiu-jitsu tournament to attend, Higher Ground took five kids. It was there Jansen discovered the kids needed additional coaches because he couldn't do it all by himself. "Three of them took gold and two took silver, and both of those guys lost to a position inside called 'guard,' which I had never learned except from the self-defense perspective. But I didn't know how to teach them to attack from that position," he said. "Then I met Coach David Reilly, owner of Undisputed Gym, who is also head coach and instructor of Brazilian jiu-jitsu there. He said, 'I'll train you and your kids, and you can all train at my gym too.' I also met Steve Owen, assistant wrestling coach from Flowing Wells High School, who specialized in judo, and he agreed to become our judo coach."

In addition to the added coaches, creating partnerships with multiple organizations in Tucson has allowed Higher Ground to expand and work with multiple child agencies and other nonprofit organizations in Tucson. The popularity and success of Higher Ground grew exponentially and allowed it to be the solution to another crisis in the community. When TUSD closed several schools,

Valencia Middle School needed all its classrooms back. Jansen then partnered with TUSD to move Higher Ground into Wakefield Middle School, one of the several schools that were closed, giving them more space and broadened community outreach in an area of the city that is impoverished and needy. Thus, the expanded Higher Ground Resource Center was born.

From 10 kids in his living room to 60 in a church to 130 at a school to more than 2,000 through the resource center, the growth of Higher Ground is a testimony to the power of purpose in caring for others, as it currently provides behavioral health and social-emotional learning to critically at-risk youth suffering from the effects of childhood trauma and poverty. "In addition to our location at Wakefield Middle School, many services are provided in the Tucson and Sunnyside Unified School Districts and the Pima County Juvenile Court Center," Jansen said. "A lot of kids get close to their coaches and tutors, then relationships are formed. We can then dive deeply into their lives and address their personal needs while teaching kids the grit principles of how to stick to their interest, have a passion for it, and how to work *through* their challenges by showing them how to practice discipline, and the skills they've learned. That's the key to everything in life in order to have hope. It's like martial arts—this is not just a program, it's a lifestyle."

Kids on long-term suspension from school are some of the neediest students, so Higher Ground offered these grit principles to local schools as an alternative to suspension. Students are assigned to go to four separate school locations in TUSD five days a week during their suspensions. "Higher Ground created the social-emotional learning piece, with two-and-a-half hours twice a week of jiu-jitsu, judo, and basketball with the students; then TUSD handles the rest of the academic instruction," Jansen said. "They enter the beginning phase of Higher Ground training at these transitional schools and experience jiu-jitsu as a way to manage their anger and their actions while learning valuable lessons."

Jansen uses the martial arts techniques themselves to illustrate those lessons. "In jiu-jitsu, there's a move to escape the opponent's grip of your upper body or 'side mount' and then turn to your opponent to 'shrimp' or contort your body in such a way as to get out and put them in 'guard,' or a protected state inside your control with your legs around them," Jansen described. "It's very basic in the sport, but it also teaches four powerful life principles."

Jansen elaborated on those principles as follows:

- If you have a problem, you want to solve it before it gets deeper. The best way to escape is to shrimp before your opponent moves in too close. It's problem solving.

- You never want to turn away from your problems, because if you do that, they get bigger. The same is true in jiu-jitsu; if you turn away, your opponent can get your back and choke you out. When you are escaping, shrimp every problem in life, and instead turn and face them.

- Your problem is not going to go away. You have to face it, solve it early, and have a plan on how to turn it into an opportunity. When you have your opponent in guard, you are in a position of attack. You can't just close your legs and win, but turn that moment into an opportunity to attack.

- Sometimes you aren't escaping, but attacking from a bad position. So it is in life; if you made a mistake, don't wait. Solve the problem now, and don't run away, because it's only going to get bigger. Face it and turn it into an opportunity.

"It's 'escaping the side mount,' and that's all it is," Jansen said. Higher Ground also brought that same training and lesson approach into other school districts to include a full curriculum of jiu-jitsu training as an alternative or replacement to PE in middle schools. "Our nonprofit uses that as we enter into schools to work with the students. The transitions we see are so good with kids who are addicted to drugs or consistently absent. Within two months, they have much better grades with focus or have completely dropped the drug addictions."

> *"The transitions we see are so good with kids who are addicted to drugs or consistently absent. Within two months, they have much better grades with focus or have completely dropped the drug addictions."*

In addition to positive transformation in the student's lives, the normal fees are $100 for training or after school sports, and this is another issue solved through Higher Ground. The majority of kids in low-income communities cannot afford $100 per month for such personal classes. The average jiu-jitsu class costs about $200, including purchase of the white gi uniform. "Students taking standard classes train four days a week, so they would need at least two uniforms," Jansen said, "but because we train at their school, it's not necessary to have a uniform, and we don't include competitions or need transportation with all the other aspects of the sport. When you add it all up, taking martial arts is just as expensive as playing football, if not more. By putting this into schools as part of their PE, it is free. This exposure to martial arts without the cost is invaluable. Kids see a side of martial arts which is often portrayed as beating people up, but now they can experience it firsthand and realize that it's actually a healthy mind-set toward competition while receiving respect, honor, and praise for hard work."

Much of this approach now being taken into schools is driven by Jansen's faith, and he says its future is completely dependent on where God wants to develop it further. As of now, he wants to be able to duplicate the way they do things through this applied social and emotional training to affect more people. "I want this martial arts aspect to be integrated into schools because we have so much to offer," he said, "but the martial arts community has not done a good job about applying the science and psychological perspective to what we do as related to brain function, anger management, and using martial arts as a tool to resolve PTSD, ADHD, and so many other dysfunctions. An additional challenge is that in the open community of martial arts, we don't have much control of the elements being used or the standards of the coaches. While extremely positive, martial arts can have the exact opposite effect with a bad coach. We have to better monitor that for our kids' sake."

"Kids see a side of martial arts which is often portrayed as beating people up, but now they can experience it firsthand and realize that it's actually a healthy mind-set toward competition while receiving respect, honor, and praise for hard work."

*   *   *

One of the many kids benefitting from Higher Ground was Barbie and Jansen's son Timmy, who spent five years as a Higher Ground student and then graduated from high school. "His risk factors were high: divorced family, low-income, high-crime neighborhood, and low-performing schools, all which forecast that he was eight times or more likely to drop out of school," Jansen said. "But Timmy went on to study music at Christ For the Nations Institute and graduated from college, fulfilling the Higher Ground definition of success: community contribution. He returned to Tucson to work at Higher Ground, helping as a child and family advocate, building relationships with the youth, and giving back to the community." Timmy has become a marine and will be leaving to serve his country in the summer of 2018. "We are so proud of him!" Jansen added.

Timmy has proven what Jansen has always believed—that becoming a better version of yourself is not the same thing as following your heart, because Jansen says the heart is treacherous. It's not fully formed, but selfish. "I tell my staff this, and I know it sounds weird in a place that constantly talks about passion, but I don't believe in it the way our culture does," he said. "For example, if a kid wants to do MMA, one of the first things I ask is, 'Is it because of your passion and that you love doing it, or is it because of the celebrity status you can achieve, or you see it as a quick 'get rich' scheme?'" Jansen wants kids to analyze *why* something is their heart's desire. For some it might be valid, and if so, he wants to help them pursue that. But for others it might just be a hobby. "For me, I still compete in martial arts to this day, but I no longer have the drive to be a world champion," he said. "Do I train like I want to be a world champion? Of course. That's the competitive part of me. But it's no longer my dream because my goal is my family and Higher Ground. Being a world champion would mean I'd have to sacrifice my time away from them, and I'm not willing to do that."

Jansen says there are a "billion people" passionate about football, but few are players in the National Football League. Kids can be passionate about MMA—watch it, follow it, and train in it—but that doesn't mean it has to be their career. "We live in a world where parents keep telling their kids to follow their passion, but I think that is very dangerous," he said. "What if that passion is not good for humanity or the community? We also make it look like passion is this magical thing. But if you find devotion and learn how to do that unto God, now that's passion. Do everything *with* passion—that's what we need to teach kids instead of find your passion."

He tries to give each child a reality check about what it takes to be a professional in MMA. Jansen says if there is a kid who doesn't want to work hard in school and their excuse is, "I'm gonna be a pro athlete," he tells them that only 1 percent of college athletes ever make it as professionals, and it's even tougher in MMA. "I just read an article about how some MMA fighters have to have a second job, and many of them can't make it. I want the kids to know the reality between following your passion or following your skill," he said. "If they choose to pursue an MMA career with incorrect motives, I hope they fail fast because I want them to invest their time in something else instead of the wrong thing."

On the other hand, if a kid's correct passion is to pursue a career in MMA, Jansen will lay out the groundwork for what they need to do and how early to start. He'll then get them as far as he can before connecting them with someone who can take them further. "This might be something really good for them because MMA is like any other sport; it has its risks, dangers, and quirks. But for some people, like champion fighters Georges St-Pierre and Dominick Cruz, they became a major influence in their communities by helping at-risk youth and doing tremendous things," he said with admiration. Jansen encourages those who pursue MMA as a hobby to use what they learn to become better people, because everything they learn is applicable to real life. "Dedication, teamwork, and the grind are things that will help you achieve the better things you like."

After helping Timmy make these decisions, Jansen and Barbie are working with ten-year-old Kenji, who has been enjoying both judo and jiu-jitsu and currently has won his last twenty jiu-jitsu matches with armbar submissions. "He loves it. He's had winning and losing streaks, but he works hard and doesn't want to do anything else," Jansen said, head held high. Kenji wants to be an Olympian and is already committed to a strength and conditioning routine. Jansen also says Timmy trains with his younger brother, Kenji, sometimes just to show he can still beat him up. "My wife is still the ever-patient mom who puts up with us when we're competing and traveling," Jansen said. "We have wondered: 'What if Kenji decides to become an MMA fighter after the Olympics or decides not to do the Olympics and wants to go straight into MMA?' We agree that it's not about punches, kicks, throws, and submissions, but about placing a lifestyle and culture into his future. At Higher Ground, we take the same principles and put them in place with all our kids."

The Higher Ground staff champion those principles and know that when Jansen says, "We will never mission drift," he believes that from a personal standpoint as well. He knows what they are called to do through Higher Ground regardless of how much money may be required to accomplish whatever the future holds. "Whether I have a billion dollars or zero dollars, my mission is the same. The only difference is the billion dollars would allow me to do my mission a little bit better," Jansen said, laughing. He has been interviewed by media and asked to participate in special meetings because of what Higher Ground has achieved, and he loves sharing the story. "But I hate the idea of someone being asked to share their opinion even if they don't know anything about the subject just because they're seen as an expert or are famous," he said. "I want to be present because I have purpose and can add value, not because I'm somebody people want to see. Barbie and I agree that we just want to make enough money to share what we want with people and not have to worry about our bills. I want to have influence, not fame."

It's been amazing for Jansen to watch MMA evolve and be part of that movement, and he's excited to see more jiu-jitsu gyms and judo dojos coming to the surface. "They are sprouting up like mushrooms, and it's because MMA caused the martial arts revival. Bruce Lee and *Karate Kid* movies were the groundbreakers, but now it's a legitimate sport," he said. "I do believe, however, that MMA has too much trash talking, with violence and character smearing instead of utilizing the actual martial arts philosophy, because that removes the spirit of martial arts. It's a spiritual journey." He says any fighter will tell you that when they are fighting an opponent, they learn that person's emotions. "It's hard to explain to someone if they have never been in a ring or on the mat," Jansen said. "But there's something spiritual about getting face-to-face with someone, when all your fears and hopes in training, sweat and exchanging blows, transitioning moves, and being that physically close become reality. There's an intimacy in that, and I feel it's lost in the marketing of negative talk."

"There's a silent conversation happening when two fighters are exchanging blows, and it's a conversation that is beyond words."

When he talks to fighters, Jansen has learned that most of them have much respect for their opponents. Some cross-train together, and he believes sparring is just as spiritual and important as techniques are in a bout. "When you spar with someone, especially a training partner, they become you, and you become them. You emulate each other. You feel their frustrations and know if their day is going bad or good. You inherently feel that energy. I imagine after months of training, when you finally meet your opponent in an arena, it's even more intense. I have competed in tournament settings in martial arts that were not in an octagon, and I felt that person's very heart, wondering if he was going to quit, or knowing I've given this guy everything, and he's just not going to give up," he said. "You can see what's driving them. There's a silent conversation happening when two fighters are exchanging blows, and it's a conversation that is beyond words."

Beyond words, too, is the appreciation Jansen feels for all those who have contributed to helping him become the warrior who trains and teaches others away from peril and toward a better life. "I learned a lot from my parents. My mom showed me compassion without condition, and my dad showed me grit," Jansen said. "If you look at what we do at Higher Ground, those are two necessary values: to love people because everyone is worthy of love—that's my mom; to teach people character and self-control—that's my dad. I recently realized it's a collection of who I am. My teachers and coaches encouraged me to do what I'm doing now. Dominick is one of my favorite fighters who inspired me when I was younger, and I followed his career before he was anybody, when he was still fighting in Tucson. He's been a huge supporter of Higher Ground, and he always comes at the perfect time."

"My heart has a special place for and big thanks to my wife, Barbie, Timmy, and Kenji, who support me through everything. And without God, His grace, and His timing, I wouldn't even be alive to know the incredible life ahead of me and my family. That's why we keep reaching for Higher Ground!"

9

Roman Salazar

PRIORITIES AND FAMILY MAKE HIM STRONGER

Roman Salazar is a small-town hero who continues wrestling through life to make his dreams come true for his family, but it hasn't been an easy road. "We were young. Rachelle was going to college full-time, and I was finishing high school and planning for college. We weren't married yet, but we had to figure out how to provide for our child that was on the way," he said, fierce determination in his eyes.

That challenge was only the first of what has been an amazing, humbling journey that keeps his entire family cheering and others inspired to this day.

Born in tiny Mammoth, Arizona, Roman grew up playing baseball, football, and some soccer, but ultimately became active in wrestling starting in junior high. By the time he was on his high school wrestling squad, he began watching MMA and *The Ultimate*

Fighter and thought it was crazy. "When they got in the cage and fought each other, I had the perception that they were just insane street fighter guys! It was different than the pure sport of wrestling. In my mind, I really thought that way," said Roman.

But after he wrestled and graduated from San Manuel High School in 2006, he started training in MMA at Boxing Inc in Tucson, Arizona, as a way to provide for Rachelle and their newborn baby boy. Through hard work and long hours, Roman quickly gained success as a fighter in several Arizona MMA organizations while working as a cable installer to make ends meet. As he competed, he admired the diversity of fighters and realized how much respect goes into the competition. "I told myself, 'I'm going to make it into the UFC' and told my small-town friends the same thing," he said. "But they thought I was out of my mind and said, 'That's not even real fighting.' I didn't care what they thought, but I did tell them straight to their faces, 'I'm going to do it, and you're going to be sitting on your couch down in Mammoth and see Roman Salazar fighting on your TV—I promise you that!'"

The combination of his amateur and professional record of 12–3 over the first seven years of his career led him to see fighting not as a hobby but as a profession, with getting into the UFC as the goal. It was surreal to him when and how the opportunity finally arrived. "I remember the feelings when I finally got *the* call I had been waiting for," he said proudly. "Literally, I had just defended my World Fighting Federation (WFF) bantamweight belt and held the featherweight belt as well, so I was moving up and down between weight classes." Part of the Fight Ready Gym team in Scottsdale, Arizona, Roman had prepared for the WFF title defense fight with a strenuous camp, he had a good weight cut to 135 pounds, and then he went into the cage and choked out his opponent in the first round!

After that Saturday night victory, Roman quickly learned significant lessons about the new levels of discipline he would need in order to make it to the UFC. "I'm at an all-time high. I just won the fight, the camp is over, and now I get to spend time with my family and eat what we want to eat," he said. "I hadn't had a tortilla in about nine weeks, and while I'm usually not much of a drinker, I was drinking every day just because I could. I was like, 'Give me that beer!' I partied hard, and it was all good."

Roman then tried going into the gym the following Wednesday, but his head coach, Roland Silaraup, told him he needed to take a week off. "'It doesn't matter that you finished the fight in the first round,' he said. 'Your body has been training for a five-round fight.' But it was weird because I just had a feeling about training and couldn't stop. I'd hit the bag in the garage and Rachelle would say, 'Why can't you just stop?'"

The next Saturday, he and his family went to Mammoth for a *quinceañera* for a friend's fifteenth birthday and were on their way back to Scottsdale when Roman's phone rang with a call from Nevada. "I thought to myself, 'Well, I don't owe anybody money in Nevada, and even though we did get married there, I'm pretty sure it's all paid off.' So I answered the call." He said, 'Hello? Hello?' It was like he couldn't hear me; then I heard, 'This is Sean Shelby with the UFC.'"

Roman could hardly believe his ears. Sean was a matchmaker who set up fights for the UFC. "'No, really, who is this?' I asked. I thought my manager, Jason Karpel, was playing a trick on me.

"'No, this *is* Sean Shelby,' he said. 'How bad do you want to be in the UFC? I know this is Sunday night, but we may have a slot for you. Rob Font got injured, and we may need somebody for the fight. I know you're in Arizona, but you're on standby right now. If you can fight, that's great.'"

Roman was thrilled and asked Sean where and when the fight was. Sean said it was in Nova Scotia the next Saturday, just six days away. Roman didn't hesitate. "'Perfect—you got it!' I told him, and then I called Jason right away to tell him the good news." Jason was excited, too, but when he asked Roman if he had a passport to travel to Nova Scotia, Roman told him he only had a passport card to go to and from Mexico to see family.

Jason instructed Roman to go to Tucson right away to expedite the passport by Tuesday. But Roman felt like all the cards were on the table because no one gets a passport that quickly. He didn't want Sean Shelby to write him off. "It was rough! Rachelle and I went there, and I explained to them that this was a lifetime opportunity," he said. "I showed them my article in the MMA *Junkie* magazine and said, 'I need to get there for this, and I don't care how much I have to pay for everything. I've been working hard for this my whole career.' The man I spoke to said, 'Congratulations! I will do my very best to get this through for you. Come back in two hours.' When we returned, this man handed me the passport and said, 'Good luck!' This was so amazing and such a huge sense of relief. I called Sean

Shelby and made the fight official. I hadn't yet focused on everything else I had to do to get ready for the fight. I just had the green light."

Next, Roman had to get an MRI on his brain, have his heart checked, and do all his physicals again—standard protocol, even though he had just fought two weeks earlier. "They were concerned because the EKG said my heart rate was too slow at forty-two beats per minute, and they thought it was abnormal," he said. "But I had to explain to them, 'I'm a professional MMA athlete, and this is how I roll! My workouts are continually intense, and I'm in great shape.'" When they realized that a marathon runner's heart rate is thirty-nine, it made sense to them. Incredibly, he got everything finalized by Tuesday morning, and by about seven that same evening he went to the gym to begin preparations for his UFC debut that weekend. He stepped on the scale and was shocked—it showed him at 158 pounds. He had to lose 23 pounds in time for his weigh-in Friday morning. "Sean had asked me, 'Your weight's good, right?' I said, 'Yes, of course,' but it really was terrible! I'm always well under fifteen pounds left to cut just two weeks out from the fight. But I told him it was all good. Fortunately, I was still in good shape from my last fight."

After a twelve-hour flight to Nova Scotia, Roman arrived in Canada just in time for his weight check. "Burt Watson checked my weight and said, 'You going to be able to make it?' I said, "It's not a matter *if* I can make it, but *when* I make it.'" Roman was still around 155 pounds when he got to Canada and knew he wasn't going to be able to cut weight like he normally would. He dug deep and employed aggressive fasting and water-loss techniques such as wearing plastics during workouts and wrapping up in hot towels. "My biggest thing at that moment, beyond the excitement of everything, was the moral victory of making weight when I got on the scale." Amazingly, he came in right at 135 pounds but didn't have much opportunity to relish in his achievement. "I sat down and people started asking for my autograph and pictures. I had never had that happen before. It was shell-shocking to me," Roman said. "I fought at the Wild Horse Pass Casino in Arizona just two weeks earlier with about fifteen hundred people in the audience, and now there was going to be fifteen *thousand* in the stadium in Canada. Just the crowd at the weigh-in was the most people I had ever seen in one place in my lifetime. It was unreal!"

After all the stress of the previous week, Roman took some time to be alone "Finally, Coach Roland and Frankie Saenz, one of the other UFC fighters on the Fight Ready team, went down to eat dinner, and I told them I'd meet them down there. I FaceTimed my wife on my phone, slowly breathed in, exhaled, then broke down and cried," he admitted. "I couldn't believe all this was happening, and we then talked about the emotions the kids were dealing with because of it all too. Then she said, 'Baby, you still have to fight tomorrow. You better go.' I understood. I had to gather myself because it was the first time in my whole career to become part of the UFC!"

The next night, as Roman made his walk down to the ring, he was listless and struggled to focus. There were cameras in his face and people everywhere. "It was so unbelievable—the octagon jitters that fighters talk about are real," he said, adding that he was also contemplating the fact that he was in Canada, fighting a hometown hero, Mitch Gagnon, who went to college in Halifax. "I'm expecting these people to hate me, but they're applauding me. They were happy because I took the fight and were screaming, 'Thank you, Salazar!' Why did they like me? It was so weird," he said, shaking his head. "In the fight, it felt so good to throw some good combinations, hitting him solid, but I should have been thinking about my endurance. I made some mistakes in my strikes, and he took me down in the first round by submitting me with a rear naked choke."

Roman sat on the canvas for a moment after the fight before his opponent came over and thanked him. "But I was so disappointed because of what I had told my friends," Roman said. "Yes, I'm fighting in the UFC, and people later said, 'It doesn't matter that you lost—it's okay. They expected you to lose because it was such a last-minute fight.' But I never *expect* to lose because I care." He reluctantly agreed that he didn't have the benefit of a full camp in preparation, but he learned his lessons. He could no longer spend significant time out of the gym, had to be careful at all times with his diet, and had to make lifestyle changes to accommodate his new status as a professional fighter. In addition, while Roman worked outdoors in the hot sun every day, he now understood he could get called to a bout anytime. "If the fight is right, I could be fighting in two weeks. I needed to be in that gym, and even if I got hurt, I had to be doing whatever the coach told me I *could* do," he said. "I'm not going to let that happen to me again. I'm still angry over that loss."

*   *   *

Roman believes that most men, and some women, have a built-in desire to be fighters. He certainly did. As a young child, he remembers why he got his nickname, *El Gallito*, or "little rooster," that he uses today as a fighter. "I walked into my third-grade class, looked around, and thought, 'I can beat them all up,' even the bigger guys. I sized them up in case we had to fight. It probably wasn't true, because I was just a sixty-pound kid back then. I may have gotten beat up by more than half the class," he said, laughing. "But that was my attitude." At first Roman wanted to use something cooler than *El Gallito* but decided to keep it for his career because it fit him so well.

It wasn't until Roman got to seventh grade that he got a chance to really fight, though the opportunity wasn't what he thought it was at first. He saw a poster about wrestling tryouts and thought it was going to be World Wrestling Federation–type wrestling. Interested, Roman walked upstairs to the wrestling room, saw a bunch of kids, but wondered why there was no ring. "I thought, 'This ain't wrestling!' But Mr. Trevo, the wrestling coach, said for me to just give it a go. The first couple of times I was like anybody else—on a mat getting tossed around and not knowing what was happening. But I found a passion for the sport immediately," he said. "I've always been an ultracompetitive person, but I like to compete against myself and push my own limits that way." Roman had early success in his first season, and from then on wrestling was constantly on his mind. In high school he also played football and ran track, but he said everything else made him better for wrestling. "I was best at track, but it was what I loathed. I thought it was God's cruel joke because I hated running," Roman said, "but, man, I am still good at it."

His older brother, Ramón, was seen by others to be better as a wrestler. A year-and-a-half younger than his brother, Roman was told by everyone, "Man, I hope you're as good as your brother." It didn't help that the siblings looked a lot alike. "I was always in his shadow," Roman said. "I'd take first in a tournament, and they would tell me, 'Yes, but your brother got outstanding wrestler.' The competition set up high expectations that I had to exceed. Walking into that gym literally made a man out of me during my high school years. It pushed me to limits I just didn't know were possible. There's something about it that instills not only confidence but pride with toughness from the workouts."

Roman's high school coach was strict in training and had them wear button-up shirts and ties whenever they went somewhere as a team. "We couldn't have been more proud to go out to other competitions and tournaments. Plus, San Manuel was a tiny school, so when our team took state three times, we were considered a wrestling powerhouse," Roman said. "People would say, 'Oh, you're one of those wrestlers' like we were an elite fraternity. Not everybody who started the season could make it, because it's a hard workout. If you can't make it through the practices, you're off the team. It breaks into a grind that changes you."

> *"Walking into that gym literally made a man out of me during my high school years. It pushed me to limits I just didn't know were possible. There's something about it that instills not only confidence but pride with toughness from the workouts."*

Roman promised himself that he would work hard and do everything possible to achieve his goals right out of high school. "But even though I loved the sport of wrestling, I was still a teenager, so I was involved in dumb decisions along the way, rebellious and not listening to adult advice," he said. "But life is an hourglass. It's going down before your eyes while you're waiting for something to happen. You don't get that chance to act again. Time just goes by."

His tenacity carried him into the launch of his mixed martial arts career after high school. As he matured by paying close attention to the instructions from his coaches, his career took off. This caused a change in his brother, Ramón. "At first, after my fights, people would walk up to my brother and say, 'Great fight!' and he would pretend to be me, sitting there while I was all beat up," said Roman, laughing. "But then he began to say, 'I'm going to live vicariously through you, Roman. You're crazy—I definitely don't want to be a fighter because wrestling was hard enough! Now it's time for me to live in *your* shadow.' It's the most beneficial feeling to know that I crawled out from underneath the darkness of that shadow. Now my brother is my best friend in life."

To earn his primary income while he trained and competed, Roman worked full-time for the cable company. "They gave me these terrible jobs as an installer, out in the sun with long days, but I just thought 'Well, I'm cutting weight—it's just an extra workout.' I've been that way my whole life," he said. "I see things half full instead of half empty. It's the way it is." He remained positive whenever he visited his family in Mexico. They didn't know MMA was a sport and thought instead that he was a boxer. Each time Roman patiently explained the differences between the two until they were finally able to watch him on TV. Now they not only know what MMA is all about but they support him by regularly coming to the US to see his fights. His aunts and uncles enthusiastically promote him. "They post on social media, 'Gallito Time! No matter what, you're gonna make it happen!' It's so funny, because when I'm in a local fight, one of my crazy uncles crows like a rooster," Roman said.

He also attributes some of that positive determination to his mother's influence during his career. She has attended every one of his fights, along with Rachelle. "I couldn't tell you that she's watched any of them; she hates that I fight," he said. "But she's always there and has never asked me *not* to fight, but instead tells me, 'You're training for a man that puts his pants on one leg at a time like you do. You can beat anyone in the world. Just make sure you're training harder than he is and do all *you* can do.'" Roman says his mother has no athletic background whatsoever, but she's one of his biggest influences. "Mom makes me understand that she believes in me," he said. "She tells me not to worry about my opponent. 'He might go out there and punch you, but even if you lose, we are all going to love you. So don't care about that part—do this for you!' She's my comfort as far as that goes, but I know it makes her nervous. I can hear the anxiety in her voice every time."

In the end, it's most important to Roman to fight with excellence. "I could go the distance or only two minutes; I could win or lose," he admitted. "I just have to focus on doing my very best performance. I feel like I have a whole town and community behind me, and every-body is just sitting there, watching and waiting for my next fight. They have something to talk about and be happy. They don't under-stand how much they push me beyond my limits. I want to make my community proud. I want them to know that I made it out of that tiny town to become successful, and I'm *not* going to be the last one to do so."

> "But life is an hourglass. It's going down before your eyes while you're waiting for something to happen. You don't get that chance to act again. Time just goes by."

*　　　*　　　*

Roman believes he is a lucky man because he found a support-ive wife in Rachelle and is thankful for her because of how difficult life can be in MMA. "I told her, 'You signed up for this, and being a fighter's wife is not easy.'" By the time they got married in July 2014, their son was seven, and their daughter was four. Roman began a new job as a coach at the UFC Gym in Scottsdale shortly after his first UFC fight. He then left his cable technician job because he had a four-fight contract with UFC and another big opportunity to fight Norifumi Yamamoto in February 2015. "I knew if I lost it, I might get cut by the UFC because things like that happen," he said. "I asked myself, 'Am I going to make it financially? I get paid five months' worth of the cable salary in one fight, so I figured I'd be okay."

Roman's first real six-week camp with training was an eye-open-ing experience. "I had to train full-time—you can't be at this level and *not* train full-time," he said, adding that he made big improvements in his technique in just the first week that had previously taken months to accomplish. "I didn't have to choose between boxing today or sparring tomorrow because of work. Now I could do it all, including strength and conditioning, every day," he said. "Everything is on point, and it is unreal!" The fight against Norifumi Yamamoto ended with a no-contest decision because Roman got caught with an eye poke three times in one eye, though both fighters escaped serious injury.

As Roman continues his career, he realizes that Rachelle feels like a single mother the week before each fight because he's gone fourteen hours a day between being a coach at the gym and working through his prefight training. When he's in camp six to eight weeks before a fight, it's especially difficult because Roman has three training sessions per day. "I come home, take a shower, and I'm too tired to even talk to her as she lays there beside me. But it's one of those mandatory things, and she embraces it," he said with admiration. "She never wants to bring it up or bother me. I know she feels lonely at times and talks to her family about it, but then after camp she says, 'Okay, we need to spend some time together.' I am so fortunate and count my blessings every day."

To spend more time with Roman, Rachelle started training at the UFC Gym. He said she liked it so much, she wanted him to prepare her to be able to fight at least one time competitively. One time, when they were watching a fight at a restaurant, he said Rachelle scrutinized one of the fighters, saying, "Look at him. It's terrible! He's crossing his feet. His hands are down." Roman got a tap on his shoulder from a man who said he was a former fighter. He asked Roman, "You're a fighter, right?" Roman asked him how he could tell. The guy said, "Your wife knows what she's seeing, and *that* means you've been in this game for a long time."

So it's no surprise that Roman can hear Rachelle's voice echo over everyone else's when he's fighting, and he's amazed as she tells him things like, "Keep that head movement going," and "Do more faints." "Rachelle knows what she's saying, and she knows the game. She started training just to get in shape, but now she's better than some of the guys in there," he said. "I'm impressed because I didn't think it was anything she would ever want to do. So what if she's great like Meisha Tate? The sky is the limit! These things can happen, and she has common ground with me now because she's starting to do it herself."

Both of their kids, Roman Jr. and Kaiyah, have grown up around the gym and think all people should be fighters or at least know about them. When Kaiyah was five, she and her father went into a cell phone store. As Roman shook the salesperson's hand, he said Kaiyah declared, "This is Roman Salazar, the UFC fighter." The man hesitated in his reaction. "Don't you know?" she pressed. "You didn't watch the fight in Nashville?" Roman says he is amazed at her admiration and uses it to drive him. "I always want to make them proud even though they are already," he said humbly. "They get to watch their dad on TV, and I want them to know that all the sacrifices I make are for them. I hope they won't say, 'Why were you gone so much?' but instead understand that I do this to give them the life they deserve. Without them, I don't think I'd be in this sport anymore."

Kaiyah is already a fighter in the making. One day Roman and Rachelle watched her during her muay thai class at the gym and couldn't help but chuckle. "My wife was taking my cardio kickboxing class, and she and I kept looking. Kaiyah wasn't backing down from any of the boys in the class. She had this mean mug on her face; she's such a tomboy but wears pink and is the girliest girl sometimes. It's hilarious," Roman said. "I don't think there's a thing in this world she's scared of, and if you ask her, she says, 'I want to be a fighter like you, Dad.'" They were hesitant at first to even take her to his fights because they didn't know how she was going to react to seeing her father fight and thought she might start crying. But when there was a break between rounds, Roman looked down at her, where his family was sitting, and she had her knuckles up in the air. "'Get him, Dad!' she yelled. She wanted me to beat him up harder. After the fight, she said, 'Why didn't you knock him out? Why did you leave it to the judges?' Oh man, she's funny," he said.

Roman says his son is not interested in taking the same path, pointing out that Roman Jr. is into technology and wants to make YouTube videos about the team and what happens behind the scenes. Today he's writing music and is a rapper as well. "He calls himself 'Jr. Reject,'" Roman said. "But he told me, 'Dad, I love you, but I'm *not* you. Everyone expects me to be like you, but I'm different. You're still my role model, but I just want to put all the kind of hard work you do into my music.' He's creating a custom walkout song for my next fight, and I can't wait to hear it!" He encourages Roman Jr. to do what will make him happy and draws inspiration from him as well. "I'll have an occasional 'one of those days,' where I don't feel like training. But all I have to do is look at my family," he said. "It might sound cliché, but it's a real positive point because I want to be able to leave a legacy for my children. They look up to me, and that's very important to me."

*   *   *

After a third UFC fight against Marlon Vera in August 2015, a loss by submission, Roman was offered the last match in his four-fight UFC contract against Cody Garbrandt in February 2016, but he couldn't take the fight. "They called me and the bout would have landed on my birthday, but I was only given a nine-day notice," he said. "I'll fight anybody, and I'm always ready, but unfortunately, my father had just passed away in December, and the authorities believed he was murdered." Roman explained everything to them, pointing out that he had just started training again two weeks earlier because of everything that happened with his father. They said they understood that Roman was not ready, but about one month later Roman received an email stating that he was let go from the UFC due to his "unwillingness to fight." "I couldn't believe it! It was rough since I explained the situation to them and why I was unable to fight at that moment in time. I figured they would understand," he said. "Cody then went on to have two more wins before taking the bantamweight championship. That was truly an additional blow in my life during that tragic time."

The loss of his father took place while Roman and his family were in California to spend Thanksgiving with Rachelle's family at Disneyland. "I talked to my dad on Sunday, and he was on his way back home to Scottsdale from Tucson. He told me, 'I think I'm going to beat you guys home.' But he never made it," Roman said, shaking his head. "We were worried and didn't know what happened or where he was. My dad was a recovering addict who had issues with addiction to cocaine and then meth for a long time. But living with us was his first time sober in thirty years, so we thought he had a bad relapse when we couldn't find him."

He was missing for several weeks before Roman's sister took a call from the state highway patrol while Roman and his family were with his siblings at Canyon Lake in the mountains west of Scottsdale. They were told his father's body was found in a ditch in Tucson, with his car two miles down the road. "The autopsy report showed he was clean," Roman said, adding that the authorities believed he was killed in a car accident and that his body was thrown into the desert so no one found out. When Roman and his siblings saw the pictures of his body, animals had already gotten to him. "While it was difficult to see his body, I'm glad that he didn't lose his sobriety, because that was so important to him. He was still fighting that fight," Roman said. "It's unfortunate what happened, and I was so bitter for a while. I didn't have any closure, and life took a downward spiral for me. Since my dad was so heavily into narcotics for so long, I never really let it affect me. But this was different—sadness and anger came on strong, and I didn't know where to put it. He was hit and killed the Sunday after Thanksgiving."

Roman's father never missed one of his son's fights. "He frequently asked me if I was sure about my career, and I know that he loved and cared for me. We were very close," Roman said. "My dad lived with me the last five years of his life and was our children's babysitter since they were born. He was medically retired with bipolar disorder but always there in support as part of my fight training camps. Everything I did was to make him more proud of me. After he passed, I wondered, 'Now what?' I felt such emptiness and even stopped loving the sport because, without him there, my preparations felt hollow." His father not only stayed with Roman through fight camps but was even in the locker room with his son right up to the time to leave for the octagon. "As fighters, we're weird about all the rituals we build, and my dad wasn't part of that anymore. He was active my whole fight career and for any sport I took part in as a kid. He was always the one I'd looked to for a nod of approval," he said, tears welling in his eyes. "With Dad gone before my fight versus Ed West in June 2016, I didn't feel *any* fire."

This concerned Roman's management and trainer, but Roman did everything possible to get his mind off his loss and into the ring. Rachelle provided strong support, but his daughter repeatedly asking, 'Why isn't Tata coming back?' made it rough. Roman lost to Ed West via unanimous decision, and afterward Roman told Rachelle he didn't want to fight anymore. Hoping to find the fuel to ignite his competitive fire once more, Roman got in touch with his old coach, Santino DeFranco. "He reminded me of *why* I do this sport and all it has actually done for me," Roman said. "I again feel blessed and happy to be here. That year was a very negative one, but I'm at peace with it now. I can't control everything, and there was nothing I could do. But I know my dad would want me to be happy and keep chasing my dream."

In his two fights since then for two different organizations, Roman won one and lost the other, bringing his career victory tally to ten by the end of April 2017.

*   *   *

When Roman first earned the nickname of *El Gallito* in third grade, he may have sized up his classmates in the event of a fight, but he never bullied anyone. He did, however, advise his son, Roman Jr., on how to respond when he started being bullied at school. "My son was eight at the time and had come home numerous times talking about being bullied, so I told him, 'You have to fight back. You have to stand up for yourself and find a way to deal with it,'" said Roman. Not long after that, Roman got a call from the school saying his son had been in a fight. When Roman showed up at the school, he said there was a line of teachers waiting for him. "They all looked scared that I was going to do something drastic. The principal told me, 'Your son got in a fight and punched a kid in the face.' When I told the principal how I told Roman Jr. to stand up for himself, the principal replied, 'Of course your son is going to fight. Look what you do for a career!'" Roman said. "I laughed and said, 'I'm a fighter, but that doesn't mean I'm a hit man.'"

Roman then said a teacher commented, "You shouldn't teach him to hit back or defend himself but to go tell the teacher instead." Then Roman got firm with them. "I said, 'He's tried to do that, but nothing happened, and there were no repercussions. This is how I dealt with bullies—I never want him to *be* the bully, to fight for no reason or pick on people. But if he tells the teacher and still nothing happens, you better believe he's going to have to do something about it.'" The principal suspended his son from school, but Roman was careful not to come off as abrasive, arrogant, or in any way add fuel to their fire. He tried to help them understand by comparing MMA to football in regards to hitting a person in the sport. "They told me that was completely different because what I do is fighting," he said. "There are stereotypes and bad people out there, but as a professional fighter, I hold myself to a higher standard and my kids to the same standard."

Later that same year, the Fight Ready team launched a kid's fight camp. Roman took his son to the venues and recorded a segment about bullying. Roman Jr. put up a little clip of himself on Facebook, and all his friends saw it on TV news segments with FOX News 10 and ABC Channel 15 as well. "I wondered what would happen if his teachers saw it and realized what bullying really is," Roman said. "Kids are suffering because bullying has become an epidemic, and it's getting worse. So during certain camps with the kids, we do an antibullying campaign and teach kids how not to fight but to *defend* themselves instead."

Being a trainer of kids and adults at UFC Gym for several years and now being a fighter on the Fight Ready Team full-time, Roman believes that some people are born with a "fighter gene" for the sport of MMA. That doesn't mean they want to attack each other or brawl for no reason, but rather demonstrate a natural tenacity that drives them to compete in martial arts. "People and kids ask me if I feel pain," Roman said. "Of course I do. I'm not a superhero, but it's something in me—never wanting to settle for second best. I always want to push myself to be better and reach new peaks." He can usually pick out the one kid that may not be the most athletic or have the best technique but possesses a hunger within him. "It's funny. I've seen kids with tears in their eyes, but they didn't want to stop, then others who have all the talent in the world, but fifteen minutes in they're ready to quit," he said. "I remind them all: it's not a glamorous sport, and it's hard work, but you can do it *if* you want it bad enough."

In addition to constantly pushing himself to new levels to become the best he can be, Roman's biggest challenge has been his thought life. "Even when I'm training and beating guys like Henry Cejudo, UFC flyweight and Olympic champion, or UFC bantamweight Frankie Saenz every day, I have doubts and ask myself, 'Do I belong here, or did I just get lucky enough to be here? Did I fall into this position because it was short notice, or would I have been signed anyway?'" Roman says those mental battles are a tough hurdle that separates good fighters from great ones. He goes from having bad days where he wonders if he's ready for the next fight to good days where he can't wait to fight the next day. "It's the understanding that I *am* where I need to be that keeps me on the path I need to be on."

Getting requests from his old high school to visit and speak to kids is one important confirmation that he is on the right path, and it's a big deal to Roman. "I walk back into the wrestling room, where they have pictures of me up on the walls—now that's inspiring," he said with a big smile. As a small-town guy, while Roman fights out of Scottsdale, he made sure to put Mammoth, Arizona, on the map.

He tells kids if they want to make it to Major League Baseball or be a football player, they need to do everything they can to find their passion in life and get there. "Our team at Fight Ready also visits schools in Queen Creek and the local Boys and Girls Club. When these kids are in the presence of a UFC fighter, they get so excited, and one of the best ways to give back to community is to share our experience," he said. "They hear how rough life may be through grueling workouts, and when a welterweight fighter like Benny Madrid shares about his life with the gang and his upbringing, it proves no matter what situation they are in, they can push through and be more."

"It's funny. I've seen kids with tears in their eyes, but they didn't want to stop, then others who have all the talent in the world, but fifteen minutes in they're ready to quit."

While Roman said he still desires to win a championship belt, he really wants to get to a point financially where he's well-known as a fighter and trainer so he can make a difference in Mexico as well. "I'd like to be able to open a gym there. Those kids don't have anything, because it's really rough, like it was in Mammoth," he said. "I was lucky enough to get to Tucson for training, but there are so many kids that don't have that chance. I want to help them have transportation and get to other places for competitions. I want them to know that Roman Salazar helped them, not for fame or fortune, but because I know how rough circumstances can be, and a lot of times we're just looking for that one person to inspire us."

"They hear how rough life may be through grueling workouts, and when a welterweight fighter like Benny Madrid shares about his life with the gang and his upbringing, it proves no matter what situation they are in, they can push through and be more."

Roman is humbled when people ask for an autograph and wants to make sure he's a good example, showing that hard work does pay off. "I'm still just Roman Salazar—I'm still a husband and dad, and whenever I train full-time in camp toward that bout, I'm only a fighter that night. Everything else is hard work," he admitted. Since working at the Fight Ready Gym, he has become the general manager and continues to sell gym memberships and personal training packages while working with others to put them on their journey and meet their goals. Within the next couple years, he and Fight Ready Gym owner, Dave Zowine, hope to open two more Fight Ready Gyms, and Roman could run one of them while he continues to fight. Roman has also started developing expertise as a commentator for WFF events and wants to do that long term. "The more people see my face out there, the more they will know Roman Salazar. I come from humble beginnings, and I don't forget that. I'm fighting for me, my family, and the future generations."

This is part of the Alliance Gym Team in San Diego and what a great group of Warriors they are!

Brendan Loughnane is always having fun!

Roman Salazar in the heat of the battle

Dominick Cruz, Dojo and Suzette...loving it!

Wilson Reis and Dominick Cruz sparring action and focus

Thom Ortiz and his Wildcat Wrestling Team taking charge of the mats

Jansen Azarias and the Higher Ground Judo Team making it happen

Paulina Granados and Suzette rolling to a choke hold

Watch for more interviews and pictures in the next two books of the Broken Before Battle trilogy!

Phil Davis and Suzette at the Forum Arena for UFC 199

Dennis, Suzette and Anika Howe with son and coach Derek Cruz for family workout fun

Suzette in tai kwon do front stance forward into combination kick

Seth Baczynski and his family enjoying this photo opportunity

Suzette with Eric Del Fierro, head coach at Alliance Gym

Danny Martinez with the kids at Father Joe's Village in San Diego for Christmas celebration

BROKEN BEFORE BATTLE
TRILOGY

Make sure to visit my website:
www.SuzetteHowe.com

Sign up with your email to receive a
special FREE gift
as a thank you for purchasing the book and
following me through the trilogy series.

There will be different updates with new
interviews, photos and signing
opportunities taking place as
I continue reaching out to new fighters
and sharing their amazing stories.

*Please share your thoughts about these fighters and
others you'd like to read about with me on my
website. Like the fighters in this book, be sure to get
involved in your own community, reach out, and
make a difference in people's lives!*

CPSIA information can be obtained
at www.ICGtesting.com
Printed in the USA
BVHW03s0152160918
527605BV00001B/5/P